Mauro Mariotti

CINQUE TERRE

Erga edizioni

The Cinque Terre and surrounding area are remarkable for the age-old modelling work men have carried out on the land, at times fighting wild nature's inclination, at others following it, against the backdrop of a natural environment very much in the forefront, which influences human acitivity and ultimately prevails.

This is why in 1995, ten years after the foundation of the first protected area, the Region of Liguria included this beautiful section of the coastline in the Cinque Terre Regional Nature Park, which stretches from the Isolotto del Tinetto to Sestri Levante. In 1997 the Ministry for the Environment founded the protected Natural Marine Area and the Cinque Terre National Park.

The authorities' intention is not to place the area under a glass jar, but to actively guarantee its protection by motivating social and cultural promotional activities to ensure that a balance is maintained or re-established between man and nature. This spirit is clear from all the articles and regulations in the Law, which differ from area to area and according to the interests identified in them.

Et haec quinque loca vocantur quinque Terre ut scilicet privilegio et beneficio vini hanc dignitatem denominatione adepta sint inter ceteras terras orientalis ripariae...[1] With these words from the first version of the *Descriptio orae ligusticae* in 1418, Jacopo Bracelli introduces for the very first time the name Cinque Terre, attributing it to a farming area distinct from the rest of the former Genoese Republic especially due to its excellent wine production. Probably - but not certainly - this area encompassed the coastal area between Monterosso and Riomaggiore. Previously the various sites and towns of the Cinque Terre were indicated singly. The boundaries of the Cinque Terre have always been fairly vague; in his "Annals" of 1537 Agostino Giustiniani considered them to extend for 15 miles from Levanto to Portovenere. On other occasions they have been identified with the administrative areas of the town councils of Monterosso, Vernazza and Riomaggiore, including the Valle d'Albareto to the north west, which at least physiographically belongs to the Val di Vara, and ending to the east at Punta Merlino.

Topographically speaking, it is easy to identify a land unit extending from Punta del Mesco along the sea to Portovenere (bounded by the Mesco Promontory and the ridge running almost parallel to the coast), but in the real context the stretch to the east of Punta del Merlino is known as "Tramonti" (Tramonti di Biassa, Tramonti di Campiglia), accounting for the land which for the inhabitants of La Spezia is beyond the mountains, where the sun sets. Since its origin the name Cinque Terre has been linked with quality wines and the presidential decree of 29th May 1973 recognised the DOC status of the

---

1   These five towns [Monterosso, Vernazza, Corniglia, Manarola, Riomaggiore] are known as the Cinque Terre because thanks to the excellence of their wine they have won the honour of distinction by this name from all the other lands of the eastern Riviera...

1 - The Cinque Terre from Monterosso

wines produced in the administrative areas of Riomaggiore, Vernazza and Monterosso and the neighbouring area of Tramonti, as far as the boundary with the municipality of Portovenere. For brevity's sake, in the guide the term Cinque Terre will be used to denote the whole coastal area between Levanto and the Isola del Tinetto.

While the historical development of the relations between the people of the Cinque Terre and neighbouring or foreign peoples will be discussed later, it is however important to note immediately the significance of this area today in the Region of Liguria, and indirectly, on a national and European level.

The Cinque Terre, isolated for thousands of years from the main road routes, represent one of the largest natural and semi-natural Mediterranean areas of Liguria. Human activity, and wine-production in particular, has contributed to the creation of a unique landscape in which the typical dry-stone walls extend for a distance which is over as great as that of the famous Wall of China. Along with a fairly clean sea and valuable architectural remains, this has contributed to a considerable increase in the influx of tourists over the last twenty years (the number of foreign tourists has actually increased tenfold). This is not so much due to a successful promotional campaign as to the spontaneous discovery of the unique character of the place, its beauty, and the pleasure to be had in staying or visiting there. Tourism, with farming, currently represents the area's main tendency, but the two are interlinked because the appeal of the former lies above all in the landscape shaped over the centuries by the landworkers using techniques which are gradually disappearing. In the 15th century the wines of Corniglia and Vernazza were known not only in Rome but also at the tables of the French and English aristocracy; now tourists come in search of the genuine products of vine and olive in the very place where they are grown, against a beautiful natural backdrop.

THE AREA

Landform and climate

The area consists of an articulated slope between the open sea and the ridge separating it from the Val di Vara and the Gulf of Spezia; this ridge joins the main line of the Ligurian Apennines to the north west, at the Passo del Bocco. Other, secondary ridges slope down towards the coast, some more steeply than others. To the west one of these juts out arching over the massif of the Punta Mesco promontory. In the south-eastern part, on the other hand, as far up as Mt. Verrugoli, the main watershed divides into two branches, one of which curves to the north east towards La Foce and forms the boundary of the hilly amphitheatre facing the deep Gulf of La Spezia. The other turns towards the south and swiftly down to the sea at Portovenere. The watershed which forms the boundary of the area is therefore a row of mountains quite close to the sea, whose altitudes vary from 487m (Mt. Vè) to 815m (Mt. Malpertuso). The steep slope of the land is therefore not due to the relatively modest height of the peaks, but mainly to the narrow space separating them from the coastline, which varies from 0.6km (Mt. Castellana) to 2.5km (Mt. Malpertuso). The main passes are, to the west, the Valico di Soviore or del Termo (538m), which links the Cinque Terre with the Val di Vara, at the level of Monterosso on one side and Pignone on the other; to the east, the Valico del Telegrafo (516m) through which the Gulf of La Spezia can be reached from Riomaggiore. Next to these are a series of secondary passes which cross the orographic section.

The inland structure is articulated by the presence of secondary spurs which split from the main watershed, sometimes in a perpendicular line, sometimes at an angle, to the coastline. Particularly important are the Costa di S. Bernardino and the Promontory of Montenegro, to the east of Vernazza and Riomaggiore respectively. Recent tectonic activity probably caused the formation halfway up the coast of terraces, the clearest examples of which can be found at Punta Mesco, Corniglia and Volastra. Behind Levanto extends an alluvial plain, on average 700m wide and

2 - Punta Mesco

3 - *Stormy sea on the western coast of Portovenere*

about 2km deep.

At the western end jutting into the sea is Punta Mesco, one of the most important promontories in Liguria which separates the Cinque Terre (in the strict sense) from the Gulf of Levanto; apart from this the coastline runs in a straight line or with small promontories and bays originating above all from the differing erosibility of the substrata. Levanto and Monterosso are edged with sandy beaches; here and there other, mainly shingly or stony beaches are periodically supplied by landslides or steep torrents, but the rest of the coastline rises steeply over the sea in often vertical cliffs. The steepest are to be found in the eastern part between Scoglio Galera and Portovenere, where sheer rock faces several hundred metres high can be seen. The steep tendency of the coast continues below sea-level, only partially interrupted by the shoreline which has also cut off the numerous steep-sided gorges which originally extended into the sea. This characteristic along with the terrace formations bears witness to the fact that in the middle and early Quaternary period the coastline was much wider. The coastal landscape is due to both the nature of the rocks and the contrast between the arrival of materials from the dry land and the sea, and the removal of them by wave and current movement. The results of this are high, steep cliffs and narrow stretches of beach where materials are constantly brought from inland. The material brought to the main beaches is basically linked to the mouths of torrent basins or to landslides, alluvial fans and sliding of slope debris, or the unloading of materials caused by man in recent times. Removal of materials takes place through the destructive and erosive action of the waves of the south-east and south-western winds. The south-westerly waves move in a vertical direction unloading their energy towards the coast, while the undertow brings the material downwards from the shore. The prevailing result is intense erosion of the sea bed and considerable movement of the material. From the other side the sirocco waves hit the coast at an angle of about 30° on average, also wearing down the shoreline but above all causing intense movement of the material on the sea-bed and after the "shore currents" they contribute greatly to its distribution towards the open sea. Obviously the presence of promontories deviates the movement and angle of the waves against the coast and influences overall the actions described above.

Levanto's beach, between the Punta delle Rocche on the Mesco and the Punta Gone at the far end of Monte La Guardia, stretches for more than 1.5 km and is supplied with sand, shingle and stones of various kinds from the Ghiararo stream and material brought in by the sea along the promontories. The small Torre Aurora promontory forms the eastern boundary of Fegina beach, in the shade of Punta del Mesco, which is supplied mainly by torrential flooding of the Rio Fegina and the smaller Rio Molinelli and, to a lesser extent, by the material brought by the sea after washing over the huge arenaceous mass of the Punta Mesco. The beach of old Monterosso, which is close by that of Fegina, is situated between the Torre Aurora promontory and Punta Corone; its stability is dependent mainly on the torrential transport of the Canale Pastanelli. Further on, just before Corniglia, is the beach of Gùvano, supplied by landfall from the Gùvano itself; to the east Corniglia's large beach originates primarily from materials brought down from the huge foot of the Rodalabia landfall and two steep debris-heaps below Corniglia and Volastra. In many cases, the indispensable protective measures at the foot of the landfall limit the natural resupply of materials to the beach. There are other smaller beaches further to the east, such as Canneto, Nacchè, Pozzale on Palmaria, etc. The shoreline undergoes more or less abrupt variations in shape: in the last century,

4 - *The gulf of Levanto*

for example, the beach at Fegina has undergone recession of 30m or more and on the large beach of Corniglia reinforcement work has been necessary to prevent the sea from reaching the railway.

The insistent erosive action of the wave movement and, most particularly the waves from the south-west, falls more or less vertically also on stretches of sheer cliffs. In various places the sea has widened the cracks in the rocky walls, causing whole blocks of rock to slide into the sea forming rocky crags. Of interest among the many crevices created by the sea, are the "Pertuso" or "Antro del Diavolo " (Devil's Cave) near Vernazza, which is about 70m deep, the famous Grotta Arpaia near Portovenere, only partly shaped by the sea, and the numerous sea caves of the islands of Palmaria, Tino and Tinetto.

The coastal rock strata tend to slide into the sea in blocks of considerable bulk which remain almost whole or break up forming a layer of detritus, and making the coast even more spectacular when the sea is rough. Erosion by the sea, sometimes linked to recent tectonic movements, has given rise to the presence of rocky crags of various shapes and height, especially, to the east of Riomaggiore where the crags of Grimaldi, Montonaio, Ferale (the most substantial, opposite Schiara), and Galera can be seen.

The small islands probably separated from the continental mass in the late Quaternary period due to the formation of canals of tectonic origin between fissures running from SW to NE. The island of Palmaria, with a surface area of about 189 hectares, rises to 186m above sea level and at its closest point is only a few hundred metres from the land mass. The shape of its coast and elevation show the continuance of the western promontory of the Spezia gulf: to the south-west it is high, sheer and full of caves, while the north-east scarp slopes less steeply and the coast juts out at the Scuola and Mariella points, two terrace formations which reflect those present on the nearby western promontory of the Gulf. The small and predominantly stony beaches, and one stream of negligible size, complete the landscape of the island.

The island of Tino, with a surface area of about 13 hectares, rises to 122m above sea level and is about 500m from Palmaria and 2.5km from the land mass. Like

5 - The Ferale crag from Monesteroli

6 - The Island of Palmaria

Palmaria's, its coastline is high and precipitous towards the open sea, with an evenly sloping scarp towards the gulf. The small island of Tinetto, although little more than a rocky crag 17m high, has like the other islands had an important historical role.

In the Cinque Terre there are many natural springs located a few metres above sea level, almost up to the main ridge, where they also are fed by the persistent orographical mists and the high level of atmospheric humidity. Many streams are basically furrows which collect the natural waters during heavy rainfall and convey them down to the sea in steep routes of a few hundred metres; others have their own small catchment basin, like the Rio Ghiararo at Levanto, Rio Fegina, Rio Molinelli and the Canale Pastanelli at Monterosso, the Canale di Vernazza, the Canale di Groppo at Manarola and the Rio Maggiore. Towards the eastern extremity, between Punta del Persico and Portovenere, there are almost no traces of watercourses (except in the Fosso di Albana) since on the promontory they run down towards the Gulf of La Spezia along the gentler slope of the scarp. The hydrographic networks, which include remarkably steep sections and V-shaped gorges, often correspond to tectonic lines or contact points between different types of substrata, and there is a consequently high erosive and transportational potential. The watercourses, all with a "Ligurian type" flow, with highest capacity between autumn and spring, and clearly distinct summer minimums, are locally identified with the term *Canale* (canal) and *Fosso*

7 - *The landslide area of Gùvano*

the shaping of the slopes by man during the course of the centuries. The *fasce*, terraces alternating between dry-stone walls and flat sections where the soil is used for agricultural purposes, have a positive effect on restraining the land and the regular ebb of the water unless they are abandoned and neglected. If this happens, as it does all too frequently, the dry-stone walls begin to give way and the artificial rainwater channelling systems are altered, triggering or accelerating landslide phenomena, which are often extensive.

The tendency of the Cinque Terre to coastal landslides is often a conditioning factor in the area: along the coastal section there is hardly a stretch without identifiable landslide areas with unstable debris accumulations. The most extensive of these are the previously mentioned Gùvano area, below the settlement of S. Bernardino, and Corniglia (or Lavina di Rodalabia) below the town of Volastra, but other notable examples are situated on the Mesco promontory, between Riomaggiore and Manarola, and above the Seno del Canneto, directly east of Riomaggiore. The landslides have fronts of varying sizes, from a few dozen metres

(channel) according to their width and capacity.

Water flow is not only subject to natural elements but is also closely connected to

The description of the landslide of Gùvano, by two authors of the 19th century (Cesare Zolfanelli and Vincenzo Santini) is especially interesting: "On the night of the 26th December 1853, in the nearby Guvan valley, a landslide began below the church of St. Bartholomew, which extended down to the sea. A shaly stratum, rich in iron pyrite, facilitated the decomposition of the rocks due to the transformation of this mineral into iron sulphate. The rock was reduced to a paste which could easily dissolve and be washed away by the waters filtering between the layers of compacted rock and a vacuum was formed, causing the upper layer, now unsupported, to slide down and sweep away to ruin in its wake the fertile vineyards, olive groves and the houses covering that slope. The pressure of all this material, jumbled in a heap at the foot of the cliff, was so great that some boulders, obviously not joined together, which formed underwater crags in front of the small bay of Guvan, were pushed upwards and emerged covered in coral and madrepore, which were suddenly thrust into a lethal environment."

to about 2km and can reach altitudes of 200-400m. They do not constitute a recent phenomenon exclusively due to the abandonment of agricultural areas; although certainly exacerbated by this factor they are predominantly caused by the positioning and composition of geological strata. There is much historical evidence of the dimensions and devastating effects of landslides.

Since ancient times man has influenced the landscape of the Portovenere Promontory and the islands in front of it by opening and working quarries, now mostly emptied, where holes, galleries and other artificial shapes remain, some blending pleasantly with the landscape.

In the same area the limestone substratum has led to karst phenomena resulting in a high number of caves, etc. More than 36 natural caves have been noted in the area, with a particularly high concentration on the island of Palmaria. Ten or so open at sea level and have consequently been further shaped by the demolishing action of the waves, but generally they are ordinary karst caves which are now in contact with the sea because the sea level has risen. These may be real articulated caverns, simple caves or shelters, medium-sized holes, deep, narrow wells, or flues leading upwards, ranging in size from 4 - 100m. Other cavities can be seen here and there along the limestone outcrop which from Portovenere plunges north-west towards Pignone. As the limestones are included between sandstones and shales, the combination of limestone and non-limestone rocks cause a network of underground passages called *sprugole* (from the Genoese dialect word *sprugà* = the

8 - *The Cala Grande cave*

emission of sap from the vine) which used in turn to cause the *polle* phenomenon: jets of fresh water spurting into the sea or from a higher level, which are quite widespread in the Gulf of La Spezia.

Several caves have proved to be important and fruitful deposits of remains from the Quaternary period: the most famous are Grotta Arpaia, Grotta Azzurra and the Grotta dei Colombi. The first is situated between the inhabited area of Portovenere and the little Church of San Pietro, 1m above sea level, and is 20m deep. It was formed halfway through the last century by the sea which opened a fissure at the bottom of the cave leading to the square of San Pietro. This fissure was immediately repaired and blocked up with a wall, otherwise the raging waves could have

13

isolated the dolomitic point on which the church is situated. The Grotta Arpaia is also known as Grotta Byron, (legend will have it that the famous poet landed there after his famous, but improbable, swim across the Gulf) or Grotta Maria Adelaide after Maria Adelaide of Hapsburg - Lorena, Queen of Sardinia (1822-55). The Grotta Azzurra, in the north-western part of the island of Palmaria, is a spectacular sea cavern nearly 60m deep. In the innermost part an enormous stalactite hangs from the vault and a spring flows from one corner. This cave, too, is known by another name: Grotta Lazzaro Spallanzani in honour of the famous naturalist who visited it on 2nd August 1783 and briefly described it. The Grotta dei Colombi is located at a height of about 32m in the south- eastern part of Palmaria; it is about 78m deep and has a height difference of 11m in descent. Its wide opening becomes a narrow corridor which opens out into a room of dimensions about 15x18m, 8m high. Of the caves in the Spezia area it is the best known to the scientific world due to the discovery of human and animal remains, and stone, bone and terracotta artefacts of high value, found during the repeated explorations which took place mainly during the second half of the last century.

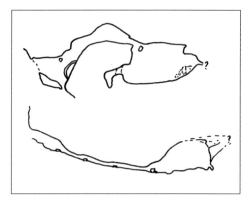

9 - Section and plan of the Grotta dei Colombi

The Cinque Terre have a Mediterranean climate moderated like the rest of coastal Liguria by the influence of the sea and the south-westerly winds, and remain sheltered from the cold northern currents. The mild winter is characterised by alternating periods of clear skies, thanks to the northern winds, and cloudy skies with extended rainfall, brought by the southerly winds. The summer is hot and dry, but towards the middle of August the rainfall begins to increase until it reaches its maximum level in autumn. For the vegetation, the understated summer drought, limited to a relatively brief period between July and August, is gener-

On Palmaria, especially on the limestone high ground bordering with the Cinque Terre from Mt. Parodi to Pignone, other superficial karst formations are common: pot-holes, sinkholes and particularly that less conspicuous phenomenon, the so-called "furrowed fields" or "rutted fields", rocky flat areas which seem to have been dug up by cart wheels but are in reality furrowed by erosion, to depths varying from a few millimetres to a few metres. When deep erosion is present, pleasant series of more or less parallel limestone vertical blade-like formations can be seen, some with rounded edges and some sharp.

ally compensated by water reserves accumulated in the preceding months. These climactic characteristics contrast sharply with those in surrounding areas such as the Val di Vara, La Spezia, the Piana della Magra and the Apuan Alps, where there are higher rain levels and the daily and seasonal temperature ranges are greater. In the Cinque Terre rainfall levels decrease and the temperature increases from Levanto to Portovenere, while the opposite happens when ascending from the sea up to the ridge. Here, as well as an increase in rainfall, there is greater cloud coverage and fog, and a higher level of humidity, mainly due to the clash between hot humid air masses from the south and the cold ones from Val di Vara.

Average rainfall statistics reach about 864mm in Palmaria, 1040mm at Portovenere, 1100 at Levanto, with maximum readings in October and November. The average annual temperatures are around 14.5 - 15°c.

The rough structure of the coastline, the presence of variously steep gorges, sometimes tending at an angle to the coastline, and local karst formations, lead to a complex interweaving of microclimactic situations all with a decisive influence on the vegetation and fauna. On a local level, the varying exposure of the slopes can cause ground temperature variations within just a few metres, so that in several cases, one can encounter a sudden change in vegetation and the presence of non-Mediterranean species just around the next ridge.

On Palmaria and on the Portovenere Promontory rainfall is strongly affected by exposure; the east-facing slopes looking towards the Gulf of La Spezia are clearly rainier than those facing west and the open sea, protected by the contours of the land mass. These two differing situations come into contact along the ridge rising from Portovenere towards the buttresses that mark the boundaries of the Cinque Terre and separate them from Val di Vara, and at Portovenere one encounters the passage from one set of climactic conditions to another, one cool and rainy, the other among the warmest and driest of eastern Liguria.

Frosts are extremely rare; far more common and at times substantial is dew formation, which in particularly dry periods can provide a source of water. The average humidity readings in Palmaria vary between 73% (max.) and 99% (min.), and extremes range between 58% and 103%. The periods of greatest atmospheric humidity are recorded between October and April.

The data concerning Palmaria shows that the prevailing winds are from the northern sector, particularly the north east, between October and March, while in the other months there is a substantial balance between these winds and the sirocco, the tepid and humid wind from the south west, or even a slight prevailing of the latter.

Rocks, minerals and the soil

There are two different geological "worlds" present in the Cinque Terre: the Tuscan and Ligurian units, both formed roughly during the same period but in different basins to their current locations, probably further to the south west in the Tyrrhenian Sea.

This juxtaposition probably originated as a result of the positioning of the Tuscan units over an autochthon or even older Apuan base nucleus. The Ligurian units would in turn have been displaced over the Tuscan units with creeping movements. The whole area can therefore be termed as a system of nappes one on top of the other caused by a series of tectonic phases, with various types of movement and sedimenting phases.

10 - Geological contact points on the "Lama della Spezia"

The early tectonic phases with considerable deformations took place possibly in the late Cretaceous period (from 100 to 65 million years ago) and in the Eocene period (from 54 to 38 m.y.a.), while in the Oligocene period (from 38 to 26 m.y.a.) sedimentation of the sandstones took place in the Ligurian and Tuscan areas and there was raising activity in the so-called Canetolo unit (or sub-Ligurian unit) which caused chaotic deposits to surge onto the normal Macigno sediments still being formed. These phenomena lasted until the early Miocene period (26 - 16.5 m.y.a.). Subsequently, in the middle Miocene (16.5 - 12 m.y.a.), new tectonic phases led first to the slip of the Canetolo unit onto the Tuscan sheets and then to the definitive covering of a small number of these by the Ligurian ones. These phenomena are to be studied within the framework of movements concerning the Corsican block, which gave rise to the new chain

of the Apennines and caused the arched contours of the Ligurian region.

In the late Miocene (12 - 5.2 m.y.a.), all of the Pliocene (5.2 - 1.8 m.y.a.) and the Quaternary periods, due to stress originating at great depth, the compressing movements became instead stretching movements; an intense vertical tectonic movement began and all those structures were generated on which the current features of the landscape are mapped out. Faults cut through existing folds creating long narrow basins (which were then partially filled with river and lake sediment), horsts (pillars) rose up on the Apuan mass and the Apennine chain and grabens (subsidences) took place along the Val di Vara and the Gulf of La Spezia. The current structure of the coastal area was therefore not caused only by vast erosive activity but was strongly influenced by the structural changes: the Gulf of La Spezia is a classic example of graben flanked by faults. Other grabens, dating back to about 18,000 years ago, took place in the continental shelf off the coast of the island of Tino and rigid stretching movements persist even today in the Tuscan-Ligurian-Emilian Apennines. The erosive action, both marine and meteoric, has had its greatest effect along the joint lines (faults in a NW-SE or NE-SW direction) where the rock crumbled more easily. The straight-lined tendency of the high coasts and the saddles located on the two promontories bordering the Gulf of La Spezia reflect these two directions.

Between the Pliocene and Quaternary periods the sea level was about 450m higher than it is today, the Vara flowed directly into the sea at the Gulf and only the summit of the westernmost promontory was visible. At the beginning of the Quaternary period raising phases led to the gradual emergence of the promontories and the formation of a small chain behind the present city of La Spezia; consequently the course of the Vara was diverted towards the Magra. In the middle and late Quaternary periods repeated variations in sea level left their mark on the inner part of the promontories and the island of Palmaria, at that stage still attached to the mainland. Remains of marine terraces can in fact be seen on two altitudinal sections, between 15 and 20m and 50 and 85m high. Separation of the islands from the land mass only took place in the late Quaternary period due to the marine erosion along structural breaks.

The three different groups of geological units - Ligurian, subLigurian and Tuscan - are arranged in order from west to east. The Ligurian units are more than 65 million years old (between the later Jurassic and later Cretaceous periods) and the

11 - *Serpentine rock*

The serpentinites are among the so-called "green rocks" or ophiolites, which have a darkish green colour dappled with blotches or alternating strips of different colours, thus giving them a similar appearance to snakeskin (hence their name). These are rocks formed as a consequence of the slow cooling of the deep magma more than 136 m.y.a. and they have undergone subsequent alterations. Their current location is due to corrugation and emergence of the depth of that ocean which in the Mesozoic period covered the current Mediterranean areas. The serpentinites which can easily be seen in the eastern and northern parts of Punta Mesco, and between that promontory and Monterosso, are, along with other "green rocks" (gabbros, jasper, etc.) part of the Bracco unit which emerges from Monterosso almost as far as Monte Zatta in the upper Val di Vara. The breccia show fractures filled with white calcite, contrasting with the dark green colour of the serpentinites: this colourful effect is even more spectacular where oxidisation of the haematite towards the magnetite gives the rocks a distinctive colour with green blotches and white and reddish veins. This is known as the Rosso di Levanto, a highly prized marble.

The gabbros, which have the same cause and period of origin and can be seen between Monterosso and Colla di Gritta, above Fegina, show coarse graining and contain beautiful diallage crystals.

The bright red, liver-coloured and dark grey jaspers with white quartz veins, are on the other hand sedimentary rocks, formed just over 136 m.y.a. as a result of the deposition of marine organisms, mainly radiolarians, tiny protozoa with siliceous shells.

The Palombini shales are a composition of schistose shales alternated with siliceous limestones and sandstones; they take their name from the grey colour similar to doves (palumbus in Latin) and are also sedimentary rocks whose origins lie in the deposition of detritus from erosive processes taking place between 136 and 100 m.y.a. under the sea. The upper layers gradually become narrower and the composition of the sediment finer, so that an almost schistose structure is visible.

The Gottero sandstones constitute a large part of the unit of this name, which extends north from Punta Mesco to Mt. Gottero and further to Mt. Molinatico. These are sedimentary rocks formed from fragments of quartz, felspar, calcite and other elements immersed in a argillaceous concretion matrix. The sediments originated from currents and underwater landslide movements between 100 and just under 65 m.y.a.. The sandstones are well-layered and alternate with softer layers of argillaceous schists forming a heterogenous deposit (flysch).

complete series is estimated to be about 2,000 - 2,500m thick. They originated in the underwater environment as a result of volcanic activity or sedimenting according to specific cases: the main outcrops are serpentinites, gabbros, jaspers, palombini shales and sandstones; the main outcrops in the easternmost part are serpentinitic breccia (ophicalcites), diabases, rodingites and calpionella limestones.

12 - "Rosso di Levanto" marble

The Canetolo unit consists of sedimentary rocks: dark grey or blackish scaly shales; limestone breccia and calcarenites, light grey and laminated on the outside; light grey calcareous siltstones and micrites with thick limestone veining, at times partially dissolved and reduced to a reddish argillaceous paste; thin layers of sandstone, also often reduced to reddish paste and at times with a certain amount of calcite; marls and limestone marls, light in colour on the outside but dark grey when cut open.

In the Cinque Terre the Canetolo unit emerges on a narrow strip at an angle between the Corniglia-Manarola stretch and the Madonna of Soviore. It includes flysch formations, mainly clay- or marly-limestone, with layers whose exposed contours show typical selective erosion phenomena due to the differences in their solidity. Inclusions (olistostromes) are common which give a chaotic appearance and indicate readjustments during the sedimenting phases. This unit was probably formed in the periods between the Palaeocene and early Miocene, from 65 to 16 m.y.a., and was deposited on the Tuscan strata by underwater landslides during or immediately after the final deposition phases of the Macigno.

The non-metamorphic Tuscan units, making up the Tuscan covering nappe, emerge from the La Spezia area and extend southwest as far as northern Latium. The series is at least 3,500m thick and at its base is

13 - Selective erosion on the Riomaggiore banded sanstones

The Rhaetavicula contorta limestones show an abundance of a lamellibranchiate fossil (the same classification as oysters and other shellfish), from which they take their name. The presence of this and many other fossils typical of marine environments indicates that it belongs to the Rhaetic formation period (a little more than 190 m.y.a.). The dark grey more or less marlaceous limestones, with a high percentage of clay, alternate with thin layers of grey-blackish marl, which alter to yellow. They form the upper parts of the islands and part of the Portovenere Promontory, over the top of more recent formations due to the aforementioned overturning.

The solid limestones, dating back to the beginning of the Jurassic period (a little more than 190 m.y.a.), stretch from the Island of Tinetto towards the Portovenere Promontory and further on as far as Casale in Val di Vara. They are also dark grey in colour and their base is dolomitized. The Portoro, a black lens-shaped marble with distinctive yellow streaks, is also part of this formation. Portoro's importance derives principally from its exploitation since the 16th century. Today the marble is hardly ever extracted due to exhausted sediments, but here and there portoro breccia can still be found, a rougher greyish marble with white calcite streaks.

The Angulata limestones take their name from the presence of the fossil Schloteinia angulata. They are dark grey in colour and arranged in layers often alternating with yellowish marls: their sedimentation occurred between 190 and 175 m.y.a.. Alternating in this formation are lenses of red ammonitic limestone, whose colour varies from dark red to pink, sometimes changing to light grey or yellow, with remains of ammonites and belemnites which prove that its age can be estimated at around 180 million years. The flinty limestones, from 180-175 m.y.a., are layers of grey-yellowish slightly marly limestone characterised by the presence of flint in the form of strips and nodules of colour which are mostly grey, and more rarely, reddish.

The formation of Posidonomya marls (lamellibranchiate fossils), dating back to 175-160 m.y.a., comprises marls and marlaceous grey limestones ending to yellow, in small layers giving a shaly effect. The jaspers, whose colour ranges from pink to red, and at times violet or greeny grey, have their origins in the sedimentation of radiolarian shells in layers a few centimetres thick, between 160 and 135 m.y.a.. The formation of majolica, consisting of whitish-grey or pink microgranular limestone, with nodules of flint, is of a reduced thickness of 5-10cm and took place between the Jurassic and Cretaceous periods or in the early Cretaceous. The multicoloured shales cover a somewhat wider space and show fossil types which existed between the Albian or Cenomanian and the Oligocene periods (from around 100 to a little over 25 m.y.a.). They are fairly heterogenous, with silty and grey marls, layers of limestone sandstone, shales and marly red and green shales, sometimes with flint.

The Macigno formation, dating back to the late Oligocene period (around 26 m.y.a.), emerging in a large part of the Cinque Terre is composed of medium or coarse sandstones in layers of varying widths, separated by blackish shales. More than half of it consists of the so-called banded sandstones of Riomaggiore in thinner layers (about 10 cm), in each of which the grain gradually becomes finer from the lower to the upper part. In the same formation are conglomerates with rounded pebbles and fine shingle immerged in a coarse sandstone matrix. The sandstones show several types of casts formed by the action of currents and waves during sediment depositing.

14 - "Portoro" marble

the past been the subject of searches and discoveries of not uncommon but quite interesting minerals. At Mesco and Fegina, during old searches for copper minerals, malachite, chalcopyrite and bornite were discovered; today these minerals are still present in the form of compacted masses while crystals are almost impossible to find. In the same area rare crystals such as quartz, hydromagnesite, soapstone, and aragonite can be found, while along the coast towards Mesco chrysotile is common, a mineral in the serpentine group with a distinctive fibrous appearance. On the eastern slopes of the Mesco azurite and interesting zeolites are worth noting. Several other minerals are to be found in the *Rosso di Levanto* quarries: anatase, epsomite, valbortite, aegirine, limonite, etc.

During the excavation of a tunnel in the last century, a nugget of gold was even found near Monterosso and on Mt Parodi the presence has been noted of silver galenite.

the cavernous limestone of the later Triassic period (more than 190-195 m.y.a.), while at the top are Oligocene sandstones (26 m.y.a.). The various formations follow on from one another in chronological order from the Portovenere Promontory and nearby islands almost as far as Monterosso, sometimes lying in vertical strata and even upside down. There are many of them, but they are only partly to be found in the area under discussion here; the oldest areas, for example, are not located here and can be observed from the eastern promontory of La Spezia, while there are crops of *Rhaetavicula* limestones, solid limestones, *Angulata* limestones, red ammonitic limestone, flinty limestones, *Posidonomya* marls, jaspers, majolica and multicoloured shales.

The area surrounding Monterosso has in

Naked rocks are visible on much of the coastal stretch, where slopes are almost vertical, but where the slopes are gentler the limestone, sandstone or serpentine rocks form a lithosol, deriving from their separation from the main body of rock. Where the rock is on the other hand softer or composed of fairly loose sediments (argillaceous schists, chaotic systems, etc.) a rigosol is formed.

If favourable conditions for further evolution of the soil exist (forest vegetation, gentle sloping, etc.) one can see brown soils, leached brown soils, and red Mediterranean soils.

21

The lithosols show only two horizons: one is superficial (A_1), of not more than 20cm with abundant organic material, and the other immediately below it (C) consists of slightly altered mineral material. In rigosols, horizon A_1 has a higher clay content and can reach a thickness of 30cm.

The brown soils consist of: a dark brown A horizon with humus rich in nitrogen (Mull type), over 25cm thick; horizon B, rich in substances deriving principally from material alteration and oxidation processes; and finally the C horizon (disintegrated and altered rock). On the sandstone the A horizon is sometimes hard and dry, and the B horizon tends to yellow in colour, with accumulations of clay easily distinguishable by their darker colour. The brown soils can be the object of leaching phenomena which highlight a clearer separation between the horizons, accumulation of clay and multiform gathering of individual particles. In some cases these leached brown soils show an upper part divided into A_1 and A_2, the former more or less rich in humus and the latter light yellowish in colour and leached. The lower part B has a strong accumulation of clay (almost double the amount in the horizon above).

The red Mediterranean soils, exclusive of limestone substrata, have an ABC profile, with a very dark horizon A, and clearly argillaceous B horizon, red in colour due to the particularly high concentration of iron oxide.

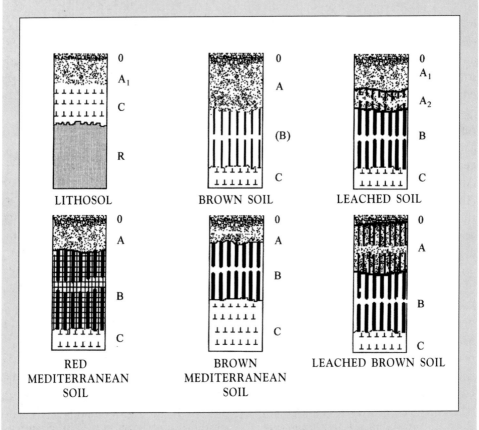

15 - Soil profiles

Flora and vegetation

The Cinque Terre landscape has changed considerably since prehistoric times due to anthropic activity: man has widely cultivated vines and to a lesser extent, olives, to the disadvantage of the holm oak woods and planted or spread woods of chestnut and maritime pine. Only the recent abandonment of agricultural areas has allowed the natural vegetation to spread rapidly, or at times more slowly due to erosive phenomena. Men, on the other hand, brought and spread exotic elements, generally without realising. The vegetal and animal species present today in this section of the Riviera are therefore the fruit of a history which began millions of years ago but which has been strongly influenced by more recent events. For this reason the palmetto, a living fossil and leftover sign of the Tertiary period, rubs shoulders with the conspicuous agaves and the prickly pear, which were certainly imported after the discovery of America.

About 1,000 species of flora are found in the Cinque Terre, a sixth of the national and a third of the regional flora. This is a considerable amount for an area of around 36 km², owing to the wide variety of environments and the contrasts between different geological substrata and between cultivated and natural areas. More than 40% of the species are Mediterranean and more than 20% are from the Eurasian continent. There is also a considerable element (21.4%) of species which are present in all - or almost all - the areas of the world, and adventitious species introduced by man (predominantly

16 - Tree spurge

of American origin). The endemic category, which includes only the species of the Cinque Terre and surroundings, is very limited. This is further evidence that the islands were detached from the mainland relatively recently, and the Cinque Terre are not clearly isolated from the adjoining areas. The high number of annual plants, which complete their life cycle in a single season, and pass the inclement season as seeds, is indicative of Mediterranean areas with low rainfall. Their presence in the Cinque Terre is mainly favoured by the extensive cultivated areas where farming procedures often do not allow the development of perennials but leave enough time for annuals to complete their brief life cycle. The notable percentage of phanerophytes, plants belonging to shrubby and arboreal vegetation layers, clearly indicate the Mediterranean character of the Cinque Terre flora. The low number of endemic species and high number of widespread species could give a rather dull and uninteresting impression of the flora in this area, but one of its greatest merits lies in the numerous western Mediterranean species, which reach their north-eastern limit in the Cinque Terre, for example, the cork-oak, tree-spurge, oval bedstraw and vine-tie.

Among the endemic species two composites stand out: the Portovenere cornflower and Ligurian lavender cotton. Also of considerable interest are some species linked exclusively or preferentially to the hard ophiolitic substrata, like Salzmann's greenweed and Maranta's fern.

The merits of the flora found in the Cinque Terre also however lie in flower species admired by anyone who crosses the area, even without the slightest bo-

---

Centaurea veneris (Portovenere cornflower), found exclusively on the Portovenere Promontory and surrounding small islands, flowers abundantly on the limestone coastal crags, from a few dozen to 310 m above the sea, and is the northernmost of the elements of the group Centaurea cineraria, all highly localised in small, almost always coastal, limestone areas, between Portovenere, Otranto and Algeria. Santolina ligustica (Ligurian lavender cotton) is found exclusively between Monterosso and Deiva Marina, on the sunny and eroded ophiolitic rocks, between 5 and 650m above the sea; it originated from a stock possibly more diffuse in the Mediterranean before the great glaciations, and was subsequently fragmented and differentiated into localised groups on inhospitable substrata along the Tyrrhenian coast, in Corsica and in Sardinia. Recently a grass species was also described, Festuca veneris (Portovenere fescue), whose distribution seems limited to the small islands and the Portovenere Promontory.

Other endemic species can be found which are linked preferentially or exclusively to the ophiolitic substrata, difficult to colonise due to their high magnesium content and low instance of nutritional substances: Genista salzmanii (Salzmann's greenweed), Euphorbia spinosa subsp. ligustica (Ligurian spiny spurge) and Festuca robustifolia (strong-leafed fescue). The first is a leguminous shrub from the Tyrrhenian area, preferentially distributed on the ophiolitic substrata of the Ligurian and Tuscan-Ligurian Apennines, in Corsica, Sardinia and Elba. The second favours ophiolitic rocks but will live on land of various kinds provided it is sunny, dry and rocky or stony (the Ligurian subspecies is found between the Maritime Alps and the Parma Apennines). The third, a grass species, is again commonly found on crags and the dry pastures on the ophiolitic rocks, but it is also to be seen

17 - Portovenere fescue: a recent natural find

18 - Portovenere cornflower
19 - Salzmann's greenweed

on limestone and sandstone areas of the Apennines and in Sicily.

Globularia incanescens (Apuan globe daisy), on the other hand, is linked to limestone rocks and is a noteworthy endemic species of the Apuan Alps and the Tuscan-Emilian Apennines, with a few examples found on the dolomite of the Portovenere Promontory at an altitude of 250m. The origins of Dryopteris tyrrhena (Tyrrhenian fern) date back perhaps to the old Mediterranean-mountain flora, and it is now found in only a few places in southern Spain, Sardinia, Corsica, the Tuscan Archipelago as well as the Cinque Terre, where it reaches its northernmost limit in sparse colonies consisting of a few clumps between 170 and 475m. Brassica oleracea subsp. robertiana (rock wild cabbage, a close but wild relation of the garden cabbage and the similar varieties of cauliflower, kohlrabi, broccoli, etc.) covers a limited Etruscan-Ligurian-Provencale area, with isolated populations on the coastal and mountain crags from Catalonia (Cadaquès) to the Italian peninsula (Mt. Conero in the Marche). Other Etruscan-Ligurian-Provençale subendemic elements are Serapias neglecta (Scarce Serapias), a beautiful wild orchid found in meadows, olive groves and in the dry, sunniest wildernesses in the Cinque Terre, and Campanula medium (Canterbury bells) whose territory covers the area between the département of Gard, in southern France, and Mt. Amiata in southern Tuscany, and is widespread in the Cinque Terre where its abundant flowers stand out along the roadsides. A Tyrrhenian element becoming rarer due to alteration of the sandy beaches, its exclusive environment, is Polygonum robertii (St. Robert knotgrass), noted at Monterosso but perhaps now extinct; two subendemic species with a more decidedly northern character are Phyteuma scorzonerifolium (black salsify-leaved rampion) and Luzula pedemontana (Piedmontese wood-rush), which in the Cinque Terre are both more common in the woods and at the edges of this summit area or in cooler gorges.

Other varieties which may be considered endemic or subendemic in Italy are: Centaurea

20 - *The thick rough bark of the cork oak*
21 - *Canterbury bluebell*

aplolepa *subsp.* lunensis *(Luni cornflower), a lovely composite which is widespread in the arid areas of the eastern Riviera, the eastern Ligurian Apennines and the Parma Apennines;* Scabiosa uniseta *(southern gipsy rose), which is found in dry meadows and the scrub all along the Apennines;* Robertia taraxacoides *(Apenninic cat's ear), a small composite spread over the stony areas of the Apennines, Sicily, Corsica, Sardinia and a small part of Algeria.*

A few western Mediterranean or subtropical species, sometimes of ancient origin and widespread in the pre-glacial period, are interesting from a phytogeographical point of view, although not endemic. Many of them are ferns, which in the Cinque Terre are among the most varied in Liguria and as well as the aforementioned Dryopteris tyrrhena, they include: Asplenium petrarchae (Petrarch's spleenworth, noted on Palmaria and Tino but not seen recently), Asplenium billotii (Lanceolate spleenworth), Asplenium adiantum-nigrum subsp. corrunense (serpentine form of black spleenworth), Cheilanthes maderensis (Madeira fern), Notholaena maranthae (Maranta's fern) and Pteris cretica (Crete fern). Apart from Pteris cretica which thrives here and there along the water courses in shady places, and Notholaena maranthae and Asplenium adiantum-nigrum subsp. corrunense, which prefer rocks and ophiolitic detritus, the other ferns grow mainly on the crags and on the dry-stone walls in the crevices between the stones.

Worth noting are the colonies of Quercus suber (cork or cork oak), which are quite widespread between Campiglia and Schiara, and less so in other places; the cork is a Mediterranean-Atlantic species, linked to siliceous areas and it reaches the north-easternmost point of its territory in Liguria where it is not found higher than 600m. Ulex europaeus (gorse) is a very thorny bush with early flowering (January-April), and is definitely Atlantic in distribution; in the Cinque Terre it is most commonly found in summit areas and in cool, shady gorges, where the micro-climate has a high level of humidity. It favours siliceous ground and becomes almost infestant in burnt areas, as germination of the seeds is favoured by fire. Euphorbia dendroides (tree spurge) is a central-Mediterranean species which was more diffuse in the past; in the Cinque Terre it is most common on crags, on detritus and in some abandoned agricultural areas along the coast up to about 300m in height. It presents an interesting aestivation phenomenon, that is to say it loses its leaves and rests not in winter but in summer, when climactic conditions tend to be dry and hot; this is a common phenomenon in many tropical plants but rarer in these latitudes. Cistus incanus (red rock-rose) is a small bush, quite widespread in the Mediterranean areas of Italy and the islands, but very rare in Liguria where it reaches the northernmost limit of its distribution. Galium scabrum (oval bedstraw) is quite an unostentatious plant but one of the most interesting species of flora in the Cinque Terre; it is a species found in the western Mediterranean, with fragmentary distribution in Sardinia, Corsica, the Tuscan Archipelago, north-west Africa, southern Spain, the Canary Islands and Madeira. The only places where it is found in the Italian peninsula are around La Spezia and on the nearby Tuscan coast. Chamaerops humilis, the palmetto which is very widespread in the south-west Mediterranean, was recently discovered on the sheer cliffs of the Portofino Promontory and the Punta del Mesco. Its presence in Liguria could perhaps be connected to the Oligocenic fossil palms, but it is more likely that its current diffusion is due to the recent transportation of seeds by birds and the general warming of the climate. Ampelodesmos mauritanica (vine-tie), from the western Mediterranean, is also here at the northernmost limit of its distribution; once its stalk and leaves were soaked and used in the manufacture of strong ropes for fishing and twine for vines.

tanical expertise. One example are the tiny wild orchids, especially the ophrys (bee orchid, spider orchid, late spider orchid, etc), with their distinctive flowers, each of which has a "labellum", a larger petal whose shape and intricate decorations imitate the female body of certain hymenoptera, and release into the environment chemical substances identical or similar to those released by these females to attract the males. The males, deceived, perch on the ophrys in an attempt to "wed" them; disappointed, but pollinated, they move away and then fall for the same trick again, thus carrying the pollen accurately from one flower to another. In this area the ophrys are more common on the limestone substrata of the Portovenere Promontory and on the islands; these plants are thoroughly pro-

22 - Late spider orchid (Ophrys fuciflora)

23 - *St. John's Lily*

cineraria or the blue bells. Of considerable importance in the Mediterranean environment are species like thyme, myrtle, rosemary, golden eternal flowers (*Helichrysum*) which release delicate and yet heavy fragrances especially in the warmest hours of the day.

Liguria, and especially the eastern part, is perhaps one of the Mediterranean areas where the natural vegetation has remained longest; until the Middle ages it is likely that a large, shady holm oak wood stood along the coast of the Cinque Terre, with small hamlets here and there and a few small plots with cultivated vineyards. The strips of holm oak wood are still today more numerous in the eastern part of the Riviera, more precisely to the east of Sestri Levante, coinciding with the point of diversion of the main Aurelia road and the Genoa- Livorno motorway, which follow the Roman road system and turn inland away from the coast, to follow the Val di Vara. In this part of Liguria where various types of natural vegetation have been preserved, the fragmentation of the holm oak woods is almost entirely due to the development of mixed farming (which over the centuries has included vines, olive and citrus groves), with the very recent addition of sparse building developments. Man has split up the holm oak woods and prevented them from spreading with various other actions especially fires, cutting and reafforestation with maritime pines.

What type of vegetation coverage would there be in the Cinque Terre if human activity were suspended and the current climactic conditions persisted? Undoubt-

tected by Regional Law no.9/84, and picking them is strictly prohibited. The other orchid species flowering extensively in the spring throughout the Cinque Terre are equally worthy of admiration: the large pink butterfly orchid, yellow Provence orchid, early purple orchid, the Tongue orchids with their long labella and brown or flesh colours, and many more.

In the glades of the woods, above 400m in height, flowers the showy St. John's Lily, with its beautiful orangey-red colours, which is also a protected species becoming rarer due to excessive picking. Sometimes the landscape's most admirable features derive from the splashes of colour, occasionally blankets of colour like the example of the white rock-roses and yellow Spanish broom, or isolated spots like the scarlet Balbis pinks, the golden edly after quite a long period (two centuries or more), there would be a return of climax vegetation, that is to say complex, stable vegetal communities, above all retaining a balance within the environmental factors (climate, soil, animal organisms, etc.). Research shows that on almost all the surface area of the Cinque Terre, from a few metres above the sea to altitudes of about 600m, the climax vegetation is represented by the typically Mediterranean holm oak wood, while higher up, between 600 and 815m, by a mixed sub-Mediterranean wood with deciduous and semi-deciduous broadleaf plants. These are sometimes predominantly pubescent oak and sometimes turkey oak, but there is also the sporadic presence of holm oak, chestnut, hophornbeam and manna ash. Some constant conditioning factors naturally never allow wood communities to evolve; on the sheer cliffs over the sea, exposed to the saline action or however deprived of all but the minimal amounts of earth due to erosive action, the early stages intermingle with the later ones: the holm oak wood will never be able to take root on those rocks directly above sea level, and they will always house a highly specialised plant community able to stand the high saline levels. Other craggy zones too, more or less solid and vertical, can house several communities, usually herbaceous-shrubby (never woods) as long as these geomorphological conditions persist, and in this way the potential vegetation will also maintain an appreciable level of biological diversity.

The real situation is very different and much more varied than that described above. About 30% of the surface area is covered by farmland (vineyards, olive groves, vegetable gardens, etc.) or "fasce" where farming activity has been abandoned very recently. Another reasonable percentage, about 20%, is represented by shrub vegetation which has settled on the strips of land abandoned longer ago, and this would tend to evolve towards holm oak woods if the periodic fires did not beat it back. Still another part, about 30%, houses maritime pine groves, ruined to a greater or lesser extent and certainly artificially planted or in any case aided by man. The remaining 20% or so, has a more natural vegetation coverage: holm oak woods, mixed woods, craggy area maquis and garrigue, etc., mainly distributed in the easternmost area (Tramonti, Portovenere Promontory, islands), where the structure is harsher, and near the ridge.

The maritime crags and beaches

In the first few metres above sea level, apart from that narrow belt inhabited only by seaweed and encrusted lichens, the crags house isolated patches, or festoons embedded in the crevices, of rock samphire, with its succulent leaves, wild cliff carrot and darnel poa. Where a little humus can form, slightly higher up, out of the reach of the splashing waves, there are also clumps of maritime cineraria, a composite with golden inflorescence and leaves protected by white tomentum, Queen's stock, with flowers coloured from white to pink and purple, and a variety of cock's foot; only on the islands and in Portovenere, the

Portovenere cornflower is also found. Until the middle of this century the beaches of Monterosso, Levanto and Palmaria were the home of fragments of psammophilous vegetation; now, because of cleaning and resupplying of beach material, many of the species typical of the seashores have disappeared. Only further up on the beaches a few examples of sea rocket and saltwort can be seen, which are typical of coarse sand, as are species preferring rubble, like cocklebur, Mediterranean barley and devil's grass.

24   - *Rock samphire*
25   - *Ligurian spiny spurge*

26 - *Ligurian lavender cotton*
27 - *Maquis*

The garrigue and the maquis

The appearance of the garrigue is discontinuous with small, evergreen shrubs, alternating with clumps of grass on dry ground and with outcrops of rocks. Many variations merge into one another, according to the geological substrata and the level of evolution, and mix more or less continually with other stages of vegetation like the rocky formations or low maquis. Among the most common species in the garrigue are the eternal flowers, which in late spring form patches of golden inflorescences; thyme, with its pleasant, heady scent; and spiny spurge, in green semicircular cushions, and many more. The most common herbaceous plants are the haired brush grass, bluish rice millet, vernal grass, rue with its heavy scent, Luni cornflower, bitumen trefoil, and gipsy rose.

On the ophiolitic substrata, especially to the north west of Monterosso al Mare, a very different type of garrigue springs up. It is characterised by cushions of Salzmann's greenweed and spiny spurge, in the midst of which stand out white Ligurian lavender cotton and red wild carnations, as well as less conspicuous plants like serpentine plantain, Nice spurge, and strong-leaved fescue.

As in other places in Liguria, the garrigue in certain cases shows stages through which the maquis re-forms, but in others, which are more numerous, it shows degradation stages owing predominantly to the washing away of the soil, usually

31

28 - Vine-tie dominated formation

nating from other plant communities, both more strictly rock-loving and more influenced by man. The diffusion of these plant communities in the Cinque Terre seems linked to the availability of suitable substrata resulting from the abandonment of very poor farming land and continual landsliding.

The formations dominated by dense clumps of vine-tie (Ampelodesma), a grass species often reaching 2 metres in height - are found up to an altitude of 200m on the Portovenere Promontory and on Palmaria, on limestone terrain, poor in humus but rich in stony and well-aired screes. These are also dynamic stages linked to the holm oak wood. Vine-tie colonizes areas of garrigue and rapidly contributes to the evolution of the soil, leaving the space subsequently to the maquis bushes. This would normally happen anyway if it were not for fires which "rejuvenate" the vegetation (ie. take it back to an earlier, but more degradated stage).

Maquis is one of the most common features of the Cinque Terre landscape and includes stages through which nature tends to reform holm oak woods from which they are more or less distant in evolutionary terms, according to the evolutionary stage of the soil or the amount of time a cultivated area has been abandoned by men. The general characteristics of maquis are: absolute predominance of shrubs, mainly sclerophyllous species, that is, with leathery leaves which are particularly well-suited to the arid conditions. The maquis is usually characterized by dense coverage forming impenetrable tangles varying between 1

due to fires and landslides. The garrigue is often enriched with elements of maquis, mainly rock-roses or, when the outcrops of rock are more numerous and the tendency towards further degradation is greater, rock plants such as red spurvalerian and stonecrops.

Along the coast on the rocky crags, especially on the coarse stony ground and debris, or on abandoned farming strips characterised by stony, well-drained land, a type of vegetation often takes root, predominantly tree spurge, a woody plant 80-200cm high, sometimes reaching 3m, which tends to stand up like a small tree. When this bush, with its regular branches and wide foliage like an umbrella, flowers between November and May, it covers the slopes overhanging the sea with yellow. Towards the beginning of summer its foliage becomes yellow and red, giving the landscape an attractive polychrome appearance. In tree spurge formations holm oak woods species can be found to which it is related in terms of evolution, but also other species origi-

and 4 metres in height, divided into "high maquis" and "low maquis", and according to the predominance of one species or another. These are certainly not durable associations which remain unchanged over time, but various stages mingling with one another and progressing or regressing according to whether they remain undisturbed or are subjected to external influences, mostly caused by men. The maquis therefore does not make up a uniform aspect of the landscape but several aspects contributing in different ways to the characterization of this or that section of coast: the rock-rose maquis, the Spanish broom maquis, tree heath and arbutus, the mixed spiny broom and myrtle maquis, the holm oak maquis and the rosemary formation.

At slightly higher altitudes similar aspects to the maquis are found, characterised by shrub species which are not totally Mediterranean. Among the most common are the gorse pseudo-maquis typical of burnt areas, especially above 400m, and the small submontane broom bush, which leads up to the mixed wood of deciduous and semi-deciduous broadleaf plans and is often found alongside bracken.

The holm oak and cork woods

The strips of holm oak wood are currently quite limited and are almost always the result of fairly recent evolution. Various aspects differ according to the diffusion of thermoheliophilous species, left by the maquis, like the lentisk, the terebinth, the barren privet and the sweet virgin's bower, or contrarily, the more mesophilous species like the manna ash, the hophornbeam, the pubescent oak, the haw-thorn, scorpion senna, etc. There are also common arborescent holm oak formations within the maritime pine groves: these are holm oak woods, with pines, but to the external observer they look like conifer woods.

On the Pozai and Schiara sides, in the Tramonti area, there are interesting cork-dominated woods. This evergreen oak, distinguishable from the holm oak by the more bluish green colour of its leaves and especially by its coarse bark, is joined by the holm oak and some pubescent oaks. The structure of cork oak woods is usually more open than that of holm oak woods and gives more space to heliophilous plants like tree heath and sage-leaved rock-rose.

29 - Holm oak wood

30 - Maritime pine wood

Pine woods

The maritime pine has great capacities for growth and adaptability and it is also one of the most productive timber conifers. These qualities have guided forestry policies in the past towards extensive artificial diffusion of pinewoods, which in Liguria coincide with the holm oak wood's potential area and the area of transition towards thermophilous broadleaf woods. For this reason pinewoods are not characterised by proper species, but, according to environmental conditions, they house the same maquis and holm oak wood plants, or those of more mesophilous mixed woods. In more evolved situations, there is a presence of arborescent holm oaks under the cover of the pines, or mixed groups exist in which pines are side by side with broadleaf plants. The pinewoods would constitute a pleasant feature of the landscape were they not (due to their artificial nature) rather fragile communities, particularly easily ruined through fire or disease. They have nearly all been more or less profoundly altered by fire; their areas have been gradually reduced and they have been partially replaced by dense bushes of mainly tree heath and arbutus, or by gorse. A pine wood provides excellent material for spreading a fire: there is almost always a thick blanket of dry, undecomposed needles on the soil, and, especially in high temperatures, pine wood gives off volatile and highly combustible substances into the air. But a wood with mature pine trees is perfectly able to react to a fire: the heat facilitates the opening of their cones and the scattering of pine-nuts. In the burnt area, freed from trees and bushes, numerous small pine shoots develop which require a good deal of the sun's radiation. After the first fire, therefore, a very dense coverage of young pines is formed, which is beautiful to see but easy prey for disease and more fires. The problem actually lies in the repetition of fires (mainly deliberate): if the fire reaches a young pine forest before new seeds have been produced, the forest will almost certainly completely disappear. If not, then diseases and parasites, which spread more easily in the higher density of pine trees, will cause considerable damage. Among the most significant parasites are the processionary caterpillar and the pine scale, which has destroyed vast pine forests in France and the western Riviera, but has not yet had a similar effect in eastern Liguria.

Stretches of Aleppo pine forest, a conifer

31 - Aleppo pine

seen in dryer conditions with higher alkaline content in the substrata, were once more widespread at Punta Mesco, above Portovenere and on the islands. Most of them have been gradually thinned out by fires and replaced by shrub communities as maquis or garrigue; on Tino, on the other hand, they have evolved into a beautiful mixed wood with holm oak.

Chestnut woods
The chestnut woods are not as widespread in the Cinque Terre as in nearby Val di Vara, where the climate is less arid and the soil is deeper and less steep. However small strips of chestnut wood can be found here and there all over the area wherever the structure brings about cooler climactic conditions. Although small chestnut woods are found below 200m, their most extensive area is above 450m where the chestnut is more commonly joined by other deciduous broadleaf trees like the turkey oak, the hop-hornbeam, the manna ash, the pubescent oak, the hazel, etc. These are mostly coppices which however still have a few big old trees and some large stumps, evidence of their ancient origins as chestnut woods used for their fruit. Until the beginning of this century, chestnuts fed whole generations in the Ligurian Apennines. Fruit-chestnut groves were so extensive that in many places the term "tree" meant "chestnut tree", but ink disease and cancer of the bark, caused by fungi, decimated these plantations and caused them to be transformed into coppices, which were more resilient, only for supplying poles. In the undergrowth, according to the conditions of the micro environment, especially altitude and exposure, relatively more thermophilous species are found like those in holm oak woods - arbutus, tree heath, butcher's broom, wild madder, greater spleenworth - or more mesophilous species like knotty crane's bill, wood-rush, wood melick. Various plants which characterise the chestnut wood however can be found in acidophilous oak forests so many chestnut groves could be defined as oak forests in which men have directly or indirectly promoted the replacement of oaks with chestnuts.

32 - Chestnut wood

Oak woods
Above 500m, coppices of two rotation

(with some plants left after cutting to provide seeds) or more rarely, high forests (grown from seed), are often found. They are dominated by thermophilous oaks like the pubescent oak or the turkey oak and seem to be young woods in continual renewal with more arborescent than arboreal individuals. However, where a more extended period of evolution has taken place, the oaks are regularly spaced and allow a good deal of light to filter through: brightly coloured plants flower on a grassy carpet. The pubescent oak or the turkey oak are often accompanied by holm oaks, manna ash, hop- hornbeam, chestnut and maritime pine. Among the shrubs, hairy greenweed, broom, hairy cytisus, hawthorn and dogwood are common, while in the herbaceous layer bloody cranesbill, bastard balm, eagle fern, bladderseed, and heath false-brome can be seen. These woods are linked to dry earth with good drainage and sunny slopes, often near the main ridge.

33 - Mixed wood

Mixed woods

If we use the adjective "mixed" to mean woods where several species are present in more or less equal percentages, we find mesophilous scrub near the drainage furrows and in the hollows, characterised by alder, hop-hornbeam, manna ash and chestnut, with a rich undergrowth of hazel, bramble, old man's beard, male fern, knotty cranesbill, etc. Other, more thermophilous mixed woods, dominated by hop-hornbeam and manna ash, with elements from holm oak woods, can be found on the limestones inland from the Portovenere Promontory and

Val di Vara (around Biassa and Carpena) from where they can trespass in small stretches of the Cinque Terre. The chromatic effect of the mixed woods is most striking in spring and autumn with the various shades of colour, firstly the pale green of the shoots and then the yellow of the leaves before they fall. Mixed woods are also those in which the maritime pine grow alongside the broadleaf trees like the chestnut, pubescent oak and holm oak; these more ecologically balanced situations with more or less pure pines are a pleasant feature where the uniform dark green of the conifers intermingles with the more varied shades of the broadleaf trees.

Synanthropic vegetation

As the plantations are almost always arranged in *fasce* or terraces with dry-stone walls, mainly sandstone, types of vegetation native to these micro environments are very widespread in the Cinque Terre, which differ according to the influences of: concentration of available nutritional substances, humidity levels, exposure and size of any detritus. On the walls, practically without nutritional substances and water, vegetal communities similar to those on the craggy rocks evolve, with common spleenworth, rusty-back fern, polypody, etc. On those which are still rather dry but richer in nutritional substances a vegetal group takes root which consists of red spur-valerian, wall pellitory, navelworth and annual bluebell, while the cooler parts are clearly dominated by wall pellitory. On the dripping wet walls, which are usually in the shade and have a certain availability of nutritional substances, maidenhair fern and small mosses are found. Finally, in the upper part of the dry walls a thin layer of detritus forms colonized by stonecrops.

The vegetation that infests crops is affected mainly by different agricultural techniques, as well as the type of crop and other usual factors (soil, microclimate, etc.). In the vineyards of hotter areas, formations of annual plants with a spring cycle can be found, dominated by quacking grass, sheeps's sorrel, yellow daisies, and annual fescue. Where greater humidity and nitrogen content in the soil are to be found, lamb's quarter, warte-grass, and black nightshade thrive. In the olive groves, when they are not weeded, a brightly coloured carpet of love-in-a-mist, red pimpernel, field marigold, borage and heliotrope develops.

34 - The dry stone walls also house luxuriant vegetation

Fauna

From the late Miocene period onwards, the subsequent advance and retreat of the sea, the spreading and withdrawal of the glaciers and snowfields which took place have brought about strong climactic variations in the area which have decisively conditioned the alternation of hot and cold climate fauna. The remains of a hippopotamus found in the last century near S. Teresa, on the nearby eastern promontory of La Spezia certainly belong to the former category, while the many findings of Grotta dei Colombi and the Buca del Bersagliere on Palmaria belong to the latter. In these caves, the bones of mammals and birds were discovered which probably lived more than 9,000 years ago when the island was still joined to the mainland: wolverine and snowy owl, which now live only in cold northern areas, lynx, wild cat, ermine, chamois and ibex bear witness to the pre-existence of wild environments and cold climates. In the climactic hardening of the Quaternary period fauna species of ancient origins survived: the Spezia cave salamander, the leaf-fingered gecko, and the disc-fingered gecko belong to genuses which date back certainly to cretaceous or pre-Cretaceous periods and are considered real living fossils. Until the beginning of this century, the magnificent ocellated lizard was observed on the coast of the Cinque Terre, but is now limited to a few locations on the Western Riviera. Finally, the Cinque Terre fauna has been affected in historical periods by hunting activity and repopulation connected to it. In the last century, between 1840 and 1846, the Barbary partridge was introduced and the species remained at length in the

35 - Leaf-fingered gecko

Cinque Terre, moving here and there between Mesco and Mt. Muzzerone to eventually settle on Palmaria until the 1960's. More recently, wild rabbits (in 1955) and boar (1970) have been introduced; the former became extinct about ten years ago due to disease and hunting, and the latter is localized mainly in the highest altitudes and the Tramonti area, where it sometimes comes down almost to the sea causing damage to crops and plantations.

There are various prized fauna species worthy of scientific and educational interest. Among the endemic taxonomic units, a breed of wall lizard has been observed living exclusively on the rocks of Tinetto, with a very limited population differing from the breeds currently living on Tino, Palmaria and on the mainland (although it must be specified that herpetologists do not agree on the classificational authenticity of the Tinetto lizard). There are many endemic invertebrates whose territory centres around the eastern Riviera or Tyrrhenian coasts, but, as in the case of plants, the western Mediterranean species, close the northeastern limit of their distribution, arouse considerable interest.

Of particular interest in the sea in front of the Cinque Terre are amphioxus, progenitor of the vertebrates, once very common in numerous Italian seas but now threatened by the arrival of polluted earth material, and the ornate wrasse, quite a rare fish in the northern Tyrrhenian sea. Among the vertebrates of interest, the observation (to be confirmed) of spectacled salamander, endemic species limited to the western slopes of the Apennines chain which runs from Liguria to Calabria. On Tino and Tinetto the leaf-fingered gecko can be seen, a paleoMediterranean

36 - *Euplagia quadripunctaria*

element localised in the Sardinia-Corsican system, in the Tuscan archipelago and

Chtonius bartolii and Roncus caprai *are endemic pseudoscorpions (Arachnids) exclusive to the Spezia coast; the beetle* Parabathyscia viti *has only been observed in Corniglia and Tramonti;* Danacaea ligurica and Microhoria caprai *are other endemic beetles exclusive to certain stretches of the eastern Riviera. The chilopods, commonly called centipedes, include:* Geophilus romanus *(endemic mainly to the Apennines area), and* Eupolybothrus nudicornis *(endemic to Tyrrhenian area). Other examples endemic to the Tyrrhenian or north Tyrrhenian area are the beetles* Euplectus corsicus *(Staphylinids),* Parmena solieri *(longicorns),* Meira stierlini *and* Meira suturella *(Curculionids) and* Opatrum sculpturatum *(Tenebrionids).* Asida luigionii luigionii *is a beetle endemic to the central-northern Apennines, observed at Punta Mesco. Among the gastropods worth mentioning are the native Italian* Toffolettia striolata, Solatopupa juliana *and* Solatopupa pallida.

Among the non-endemic invertebrates of interest are: the mould-beetle Cartodere separanda *(a western Mediterranean species in the north eastern limit of its area), the nest-beetle* Parabathyscia wollastonii *(in Italy found only in Liguria), the Curculionid* Exapion ulici *(rare species biologically linked to gorse), the hemipteran* Acrosternum millierei *(very rare in Italy), the very rare butterfly* Charaxes jasius *(beautiful Mediterranean butterfly linked to arbutus),* Gonepteryx cleopatra, Axia margarita, Euplagia quadripunctaria *and* Polyommatus hispanus, *the very rare ant,* Smithistruma tenuipilis *and the gastropod* Argnia biplicata biplicata *(observed in caves in the Spezia area).*

in several small islands scattered between Tunisia, Liguria and Provence. There are many rare and interesting birds: the red-rumped swallow, the red-legged partridge, the blue rock thrush, the raven, the pallid swift, the shag, the eider duck, the peregrine falcon, all localized in the less accessible areas of the section of coast which from Riomaggiore leads to Portovenere, on the islands of Palmaria and Tino or also on the Mesco promontory.

37 - The eider duck
38 - The red-legged partridge

The environments

The Cinque Terre and neighbouring promontories of Portovenere and Punta Mesco host an extremely rich variety of marine environments and some of the most important in Liguria, comparable to Portofino and Capo Noli; they have been observed since 1982 by the Natural Marine Reserve Institution. From the rocks of Tinetto as far as Levanto limestone cliffs alternate with sandy seabeds, fine or coarse stony or sandy cliffs and seabeds, arenaceous and ophiolitic cliffs. On the cliffs, especially the limestone cliffs, the strip between the high tide level and that reached continually by spray often appears black in colour due to the abundance of single cell seaweed and encrusting or endolithic lichens

(that is, those lichens which penetrate the rocks). In the section including the high and low tide levels, the most common animals are gastropods like *littorine*, lamellibranchiates like limpets and mussels, barnacles like sea acorn.

The area underneath is more developed, which extends to 40-50m in depth: here the light allows a particularly rich and varied seaweed community to develop, with *Cistoseire*, corallines, and other types. There are innumerable animal organisms, which are predominantly invertebrates: sea acorn, sponges, actiniae, ophiurans, starfish, gastropod shellfish, sea-urchins, beautiful flatworms and nudibranchs with extraordinary luminescence and colour. In the indentations grouper, octopus and other typical "rock fish" are hidden away, like scorpion fish and blenny, while gilthead, salpa, wrasse, saddled bream and blunt-headed holifish roam in groups. Lower down, where the light fades, the animals prevail over the seaweed and are greater in size: large sponges and sea-fans like candelabras. The sandy seabeds up to about 40m deep are covered with stretches of typical Mediterranean underwater Posidonia greenery; this superior plant loses its ribbon-like leaves in winter. Near the mouths of the watercourses, where the sediment is much finer, Posidonia is replaced by another plant with narrower leaves, *cimodocea*. The Posidonia bed environment is rich in numerous vegetal and animal species and presents one of the best defence mechanisms against coastal erosion due to the mass of leaves and rhizomes which are able to partially slow down the waves' energy. Unfortunately some fishing techniques (trawling) and pollution have let to the ruin and fragmentation of this environment.

Below 35-40m where the light fades and disappears, is the pre-corallogenic and corallogenic concretions community, whose name does not, as it may seem, derive from red coral but from the predominance of red, more or less encrusted seaweed, corallines, which include red and green seaweed - poorly calcified - sea fans, large sponges and bryozoans with marvellous wefts. Typical inhabitants of the corallogenic community are red blunt-headed holifish, starfish, sea urchins, ascidia. Deeper still the seaweed disappears and animals better suited to mostly muddy seabeds prevail.

The bird-population strictly connected to the sea and its resources is also interesting: on the open sea shearwaters and storm petrels can be seen and occasionally northern gannets and puffins. On the coast one may encounter the lesser black-backed gull, the sandwich, the rare polar tern and the black cormorant; however the yellow-legged gull dominates the rocks and sea unchallenged, nesting in numerous points in the area.

On the rocks and sheer coastline rising vertically over the sea, the extremely difficult conditions, owing to the high level of salt, considerable temperature variations and almost total absence of earth, prevent the survival of all but a few plant species: the rock samphire (local name *bazie*), the Queen's stock, maritime cineraria and a few tenacious grass species.

Higher up on the rocky walls where salinity is no longer an inhibiting factor but difficulties remain due to the extremely sheer faces and absence of earth, tree-

39 - Scorpion fish, a typical craggy fish
40 - An aspect of the Posidonia bed
41 - Parazoanthus, a typical element of the
corallogenic concretions

spurge, barren privet, agaves and here and there, clumps of grass take root. There is nesting activity on some coastal sections, almost inaccessible to men, of birds like the blue rock thrush, the raven and the peregrine falcon, who require undisturbed areas and for this reason are grower rarer in this country. The recent abandonment of quarrying activity has provided these individuals and various bat species with greater local habitat possibilities in the old caves here and there in the eastern-most area. The various types of maquis include a large number of plants which depend on insects and birds for pollination and dissemination respectively. In many cases the lives of birds and insects are closely connected to those of one or a few plant species: the two-tailed pasha butterfly (arbutus), the gorse curculionid, the terebinth galls aphid, various butter-flies and umbelliferous plants like the fennel swallowtail, etc. As far as concerns transportation of pollen, the close collaboration between orchid and hymenopteran species has already been mentioned but this group of insects (particularly bees and bumblebees) pollinates the main plants of the maquis: rock-roses, tree heath, tree-spurge and many labiates like oregano, thyme and rosemary.

The continual mosaic of maquis and garrigue on one side and farming areas (both abandoned and otherwise) on the other causes a rich complex of edges or variations between one type of environment and another, which favours the presence of many bird species; these find abundant food supplies both among farming products (olives, grapes, etc.) and bushes, shrubs and wild trees (hawthorn

42 - Rocky environments
43 - The arbutus

44

44 - *The brimstone, one of the most common butterflies of the maquis*
45 - *The inside of a holm oak wood*

berries, juniper berries, blackberries, acorns, etc.). The subalpine warbler, the Sardinian warbler, and the orphean warbler all favour the sunniest maquis, olive groves and pine or holm oak woods provided they are well-spaced, while chaffinches, green finches, sparrows, robins, starlings and goldfinches are more ubiquitous and tend to frequent farmlands and abandoned areas. Among the reptiles, geckos, wall lizards, green lizards, slowworms and whip snakes are fairly common; here and there where more water is available in the torrential furrows, the ringed snake can be found hunting amphibians like tree frogs and green frogs. These small animals along with micro mammals like dormice, voles, moles, etc. constitute the greater percentage of the

46 - *The Coal tit*

diet of medium-sized carnivores: fox, badger, weasel, stone-marten, buzzard, little owl, barn owl, and the rarer harrier eagle. In the maquis and the fallow areas one is likely to see pheasant and tracks of boar, neither of which are native fauna species but were imported several decades ago for hunting, and both of which have difficulty in integrating into the delicate balance between human presence and natural environment.

The holm oak wood is a shadier, cooler environment less subject to temperature variations; moreover when it reaches a sufficient level of maturity, it permits considerable evolution of the soil and favours the development of all those or-ganisms living in direct relation to the earth, like fungi and interstitial fauna. In pine woods, on the other hand, the soil is less evolved with an abundant layer of undecomposed needles and scarce humus. The generally dense undergrowth of the holm oak wood favours the settlement of photophygous animals and birds preferring more restricted spaces: jays, cuckoos, blackbirds, great tits, etc. Among the micro mammals, dormice and the tiny Etruscan shrew can be seen, which are not however exclusive to this environment. Not infrequently, boars shelter in the denser holm oak woods and towards evening approach crops and fallow land looking for roots and tubers. The holm oak wood fauna is all in all quite poor with the exception of that living in the earth, under the stones and in the bark of old trees. The stretches of cork woods are considerably richer in terms of fauna, as their more open structure permits greater light penetration and development of grass and shrub layers, which in turn favour the settlement of animals native to woody environments and maquis.

The maritime pine woods, despite not being entirely natural botanically, are also rich in animal species: squirrels, dormice, badgers and foxes are the most common mammals, while the most frequently seen birds include the greater spotted woodpecker, the coal tit, wryneck and tree creeper. The lesser density of the arboreal layer in pine woods and cork woods also favours the butterfly population which, in the hottest hours of spring and summer, bestow an element of colour and movement on these environments.

Most deciduous woods (chestnut, turkey oak, pubescent oak, etc.) are dominated by coppices and this causes a lack of ecological niches - compared to well-structured high forests, with trees of different age groups, ancient individuals, etc. - and consequently less diversified fauna. Examples of fairly large chestnuts, however, are not totally absent, remaining from now-abandoned plantations, and these house more demanding animals. The soil of these woods with a certain amount of humus, are cooler and damper than holm oak and pine woods, and this favours the growth of fungi and microfauna. Where the woods are more openly spaced, the grassy layer shows conspicuous and abundant flowers which attract a large number of butter-flies, hymenopterans and phytophagous insects. Along the drainage lines one is not unlikely to find amphibians like the crested newt, the common toad and the Apennine stream-frog; the most common reptiles are slow-worms, the ringed snake and the long Aesculapian snake. The bird-population is richer in less dense forests, with age-old or very large trees: most frequent are the nuthatch, green woodpecker, greater spotted woodpecker, great tit, blue tit, blackbirds, blackcaps, robins, jays, wrens, tawny owls, barn owls. The sunnier glades and areas regularly cut down are frequented by the same species and the maquis, Sardinian and subalpine warbler, blackcap, etc.; on some large chestnuts the buzzard will perch, and at times, nest. The mammals are also the same as those in the pine and holm oak woods, although with considerably fewer squirrels.

The caves of this area, especially those on the Portovenere Promontory and the islands are the home of troglodytic animals (those which predominantly or exclusively live in underground caves). The presence of the Spezia cave salamander is interesting, as is that of some beetles specially adapted to living in the dark. In many grottoes and caves bats shelter (greater horseshoe bat, lesser horseshoe bat), and occasionally nocturnal birds of prey like the scops owl, barn owl and tawny owl.

MAN, HISTORY AND THE BUILT UP LANDSCAPE

PreRoman period

In the Caverna dei Colombi on Palmaria evidence has been found of the oldest, richest and most significant human presence in the eastern Riviera: however, the deposits have been moved around and therefore it is not possible to date the remains exactly and ascertain whether the cave was inhabited by men in the Palaeolithic period. The remains include male adult skulls, children's jaw-bones, various vertebra, rib-bones, parietal bones, tibia and ulna from young people and adults, fossilised mammal bones (lynx, bear, wild cat, deer, ox - perhaps urus - sheep, goat, etc), a few bones from corvine birds and pigeons, very few from fish, many sea and earth shells. Hundreds of artefacts made from flint and red jasper were also found (arrowheads, knives, scrapers, striking and smoothing implements), pieces of bones fashioned into pointed tools or daggers, ornaments (teeth and shells with holes in them), etc. Some of the fossilised remains and artefacts which are now preserved in museums in La Spezia and Florence, have been tentatively attributed to hunters and farmers living in the later Palaeolithic period

47 - Communication lines and noteworthy points of the preroman period

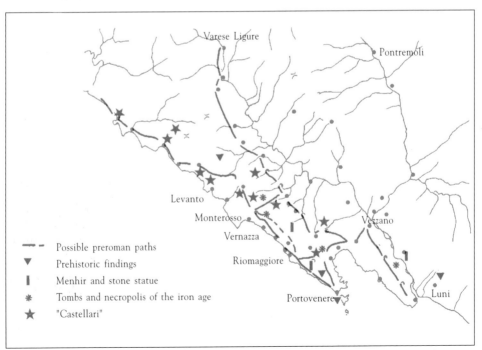

- ‑‑ ‑ Possible preroman paths
- ▼ Prehistoric findings
- ❙ Menhir and stone statue
- ✳ Tombs and necropolis of the iron age
- ★ "Castellari"

(30,000 - 10,000 years BC) when the island was still attached to the mainland. The cave was also certainly used for burial purposes in the early metal age (Aeneolithic: 3,000 - 2,000 BC) when the island was detached. The evidence of the Neolithic period (5,000 - 3,000 years BC) on the other hand, includes smoothed axes made from a particular green stone, nephrite, originating in the serpentine outcrops of eastern Liguria.

All this information leads to the conclusion that hunting, favoured by the widespread forest environments rich in game, was a primary source of resources for thousands of years, probably still in the Roman era, alongside which pastoral farming (cattle, sheep, pigs) and arable farming (barley, wheat, spelt) gradually developed, remaining however of lesser importance.

The *menhir* are certainly ancient but not easy to date; the role of these large stones fixed vertically into the earth was calendary or anthropomorphic portrayal. One can be seen in the Tramonti area, near the Cappella di S. Antonio and another is on the crest near Mt. Capri. In the Bronze Age (around 1,400 - 1,200 BC) a social organisation developed like in other areas of Liguria. The central elements, *vici*, were grouped into small autonomous districts (*pagi*) which were governed by the *castella* or *castellieri*, situated on the hills with a primarily defensive function. The lands located on the ridges made up the *Compascuum*, commonly available to the pagi in a kind of *ante litteram* cooperative, evidence of which can still be seen today in the *comunaglie* (municipal land designated for common use). The nearest *castelliere* to the Cinque Terre among those so far identified is situated in Valle di Pignone on Mt. Castellaro; the excavations here have brought to light a large number of fragments of decorated ceramic vases, indicating a stable and significant settlement.

The *pagense* organisation remained until the period in which the Romans ended their conquest of the Ligurians in 177 BC, the year in which the Luni colony was formed. However Ligurian habits and traditions probably continued even longer in the Cinque Terre, a rough and unappetising land for the Romans who certainly preferred the more productive Magra plain. The stone cists (typically Ligurian tombs) found on Mt. Soviore above Monterosso and on Mt. S. Croce above Vernazza date back to the 2nd century BC.

Many hypotheses have been formed regarding the main lines of communication used in the preRoman era, and it is likely that two routes exist. The first, probably used for transporting materials and farming-related activities, leads from Portovenere across the Cinque Terre halfway up the coast proceeding below today's *Via dei Santuari*. The second probably led along the ridge, for faster travelling and hunting activity. These longitudinal stretches were transversely linked to the *castellari*, which were distributed further back along the Pegazzano-Pignone-Mt. Bardellone-Montale di Levanto route. It is not unlikely that a landing-place, and therefore local maritime traffic, existed in the preRoman period at Vernazza.

Roman period

On reaching the eastern limits of the Cinque Terre the Romans probably rejected a real conquest of the impracticable terrain and concentrated their activities in the *Agro lunense*, the most important ancient town of Luni (or Luna), where there is a great deal of archaeological evidence. The Ligurian *pagense* organisation therefore continued in relative autonomy during Roman rule and after, until the late Middle Ages when it was engulfed by the religious organisation of "parishes" and episcopal fiefdoms. However the Romans had considerable interest in Portovenere, whose origins have been traced back to the period of Roman rule. Portovenere was mentioned by Strabone in 50 BC, and it was primarily a harbour town used for loading portoro marble which was perhaps quarried even then. There would also have been noble villas like Seno di Varignano traces of which remain today.

Greatly debated is the identification (or otherwise) of the *vinum lunense* praised by Pliny as the mellow wine of the Cinque Terre, and consequently the fact that wine was extensively produced in this part of the Riviera in the Roman era, but no definitive conclusion has been reached even today. Also uncertain is the identification of the place names Monterosso, Vernazza and Corniglia, with *Rubra*,

48 - *Plan of the Villa del Varignano: a reconstruction of the 3rd building phase (2nd half of the 1st AD). a: atrium, h: hortus (garden), c: cavaedium (court), t: torcularium (pressing room), o: oilcellar*

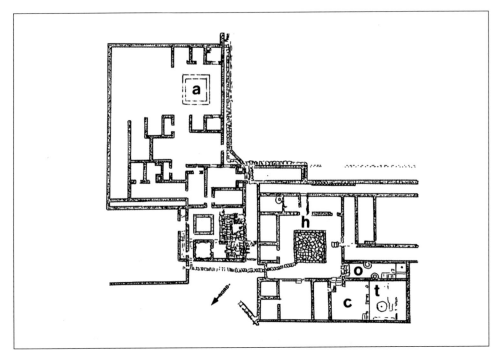

Bulnetia (or *Vulnetia*) and *Cornilium*; one school of thought dates them back to Roman terms while others identify them as local place names linked to the shape of the terrain or emerging artefacts.

For centuries the Romans preferred to avoid the eastern Riviera coast, moving from Luni towards the Po plain. In 109 BC the consul Emilio Scauro had a road built (*Aemilia Scauri*) to Piacenza joining the Via Postumia; this road led to Dertona, and, by taking another road built by the same consul, to the sea at the western Riviera at Vado Ligure. However a secondary branch probably existed which followed the bottom of the Vara valley inland as far as Pignone and Soviore. This branch, continuing from Brugnato to Genoa, gave rise to the road known - incorrectly - as the via Aurelia. It is possible that in Augustus Caesar's reign, some of the population of Liguria abandoned the inconvenient mountain locations to join Roman colonies and work on farms which had developed round the city of Luni, but when the Roman Empire ended, around the 5th century, following famines and earthquakes, there was a return to the hills and mountainous areas where farming, although carried out with primitive means, guaranteed survival. This exodus was exacerbated in the subsequent centuries by the invasions of barbaric Goths, Byzantine and Longobard rule, and invasions and vandalism by the Saracens based in Corsica and Provence.

49 - The Tinetto islet with ruins of a Byzantine settlement

The Middle Ages

Eastern monks almost certainly arrived in the 6th century with the Byzantine army and built a church on the island of Tino where holy relics were to be preserved, brought to safety from the threats of imminent invasion by Vandals and Arabs. According to some authors, today's Reggio Sanctuary, above Vernazza, was erected as a parish church defending the Byzantine border; at Soviore, above Monterosso, another Byzantine religious centre was probably destroyed in 644 by King Rotari's Longobards. Until the 10th century, when the Longobard invasions had ended, a parish church organisation was established, whose principal centres (parishes) were situated in Marinasco - near La Spezia -, Pignone and Ceula (now Montale) near Levanto. The parish boundaries initially followed those of the PreRoman *pagi* (the easternmost part of the Cinque Terre being

50 - *The Romanesque cloister on Tino*
51 - *Levanto's medieval castle*

dependent on the parish of Marinasco, and Vernazza and Monterosso on the parish of Pignone); subsequently a more widespread organisation formed with parishes in Montale, Monterosso, Vernazza, Corniglia, Riomaggiore and Portovenere. This brought about the reinforcement of Christianity and the definitive defeat of any remaining paganism hiding away in the area.

In 950 the Hubert's march, with Luni as its capital, included the eastern Riviera and consequently the Cinque Terre. The Saracen threat did not initially permit development along the coast and the population was principally distributed in the more inland towns (Soviore, Reggio, Volastra, etc.). However at the beginning of the 11th century a castle already existed in Vernazza, evidence of military activity which over a few years provided defence from the Saracens and favoured the subsequent growth of the seafaring towns Vernazza and Monterosso.

In the 11th century the monastery of St. Venerio on the island of Tino, refounded in 1056 by the Benedictines, acquired great importance; following repeated donations it became the owner of the three islands and of lands near Portovenere, Levanto, Moneglia and even in Corsica. It was an important impulse point for farming and dictated the rules for olive, vine and fig growing. The rest of the land was owned by various feudal lords: the marquesses of Massa-Corsica, the lords of Vezzano, Lavagna, Carpena, Ponzò, Corvara and Ripalta, the bishop-counts of Luni, etc. Feudal and religious organisation helped to vitalize the Cinque Terre, but the definitive configuration of the individual towns took shape from the 12th century, when the area's history walked hand in hand with Genoa's. The monastery on Tino underwent a period of decadence characterized by episodes of debauchery to the extent that halfway through the 13th century the Benedictines were temporarily replaced by Augustinian monks.

In 1113 Genoa occupied Portovenere, then consisting of a few houses and a small church, but strategically placed on the eastern borders of Genoese rule: soldiers and workmen moved there to build the first fortifications, and not long after, a larger church dedicated to St. Lawrence. In 1139 Genoa formally purchased Portovenere from the lords of Vezzano and began building a long terrace of fortress-houses in accordance with strict regulations; reinforcement of the town continued with the erection of the walls and the new castle until the 16th century.

Genoa probably exercised power over Monterosso, at the other end of the Cinque Terre, from the beginning of the 11th century, although it was officially a fiefdom which passed through the hands of the families of Da Passano, Fieschi and Malaspina. The first written document of 1132 names Levanto as a fiefdom of the noble Da Passano family, given over to Genoa as proof of their sworn loyalty.

In 1182 Genoa expunged Vernazza and occupied the *Castrum* (castle) after this maritime village, ruled by the lords of Ponzò and Corvara, had for years carried out raids on the sea to the detriment of Genoese and Pisan trade. In 1207 Vernazza declared itself subject to Genoa and solemnly promised to march with all its men when required, which then happened in

The notary Giovanni di Giona's documentation, preserved among the papers of the monastery of St. Venerio del Tino, provides a picture of life in Portovenere in the 13th century: the men of this fortified town take part in the defence of the castles, not only in Liguria but also in Cagliari, in Sardinia, and in the activities of the Genoese fleet. Genoa's cargo ships, pro comuni Ianue fleets, are attacked and robbed even in distant seas; during some periods Portovenere plays an active role in the struggle against the enemy fleets of Charles d'Anjou and the pirate ships constantly roaming the Ligurian-Provençal area, and in 1274 Palmaria is sacked by Anjou's fleet. Portovenere was a walled town with two inhabited centres: one a little older, the castrum vetus and church of St. Peter, and the other, the Genoese colony, round the castrum novum and church of St. Lawrence. As well as native locals, there were immigrants from Carpena, Framura, or more distant towns; for trade reasons there were also immigrants from Sarzana, Florence, Lucca, Rome, Pontremoli, Piacenza, Cremona, Bergamo and, despite the political tensions, even Pisa. There was a private grammar school, attended, like a college, by pupils from the coastal and immediate inland areas, where various crafts handed down from father to son were practised (scribes, notaries, doctors, shipwrights, calkers, stonecutters, shoemakers,

tailors, coopers, spinners, gunsmiths, masons, fishermen, boatmen, millers, barbers, fabric merchants, apothecaries, bakers, tavern-keepers, butchers and even a furrier). The most widely practised activities were however farming and sea trading: vines in particular, and olives to a lesser extent, were cultivated; here and there fig trees, chestnut trees and small vegetable gardens were planted for domestic requirements; flowering woods with tall trees adorned the Spezia coast and some areas were used for pasture. On the sea, locally built vessels of varying styles and sizes were used, which were almost always suitable for coasting along the Tyrrhenian coast to the ports of Piombino, Montalto, Pisa, Grosseto, Corneto, Rome, Naples, Castellammare, Calabria, Sicily, Sardinia and Corsica. The cargoes were wheat, millet, barley, wine, Sardinian livestock, salt, iron, coal, fabrics, arms. Money from land activities was invested in sea trade and almost the whole town had a financial interest in it, suffering some losses but more often reaping the benefits.

This picture of Portovenere can be applied, with small variations, to the whole Cinque Terre area.

52 - The capitular tower of Portovenere

1210 when the Pisans attacked and sacked Portovenere. Vernazza and Portovenere, now under Genoese rule, thanks to the much-admired maritime expertise of their men, enjoyed the privilege of electing a deputy without whose presence in Genoa no war action could be decided.

In 1251 on Mt. Vergiona (probably today's Verrugoli) the inhabitants of the villages from Riomaggiore to La Spezia swore loyalty to Genoa in the war against Pisa for possession of Lerici. 1276 saw enforced the definitive submission of the Cinque Terre to the Republic of Genoa: Nicolò Fieschi, count of Lavagna, was stripped of all rights to the "castelli" of Riomaggiore, Manarola, Corniglia, Vernazza, Volastra, Biassa, Montale and Carpena.

In the 12th and 13th centuries the tendency was to subdivide land property and there was an increase in farming areas which probably signals the beginning of the characterization of the Cinque Terre landscape with a shape similar to that which we see today: extended terracing with vineyards and olive groves, chestnut woods for their fruit, timber woods. Construction of the terracing, following considerable and progressive deforestation, must have been remarkably labourious. Relations with Genoa allowed the area to be inserted into an advantageous trading network and a flourishing financial organisation favouring investments, trade in farming produce (principally wine, which soon acquired a well-deserved fame) and availability of cereals. Many men served in the Genoese fleet: Vernazza in particular, then the most populated of the towns, provided adept sailors and when neces-

53 - *The ruins of the monastery of S. Antonio del Mesco*

sary, ships of which it owned a large number. In the second half of the 14th century a further extension of the cultivated terraces took place, but farming was on a par with other activities like fishing and trade.

The beginning of the 14th century was a magnificent period for the churches of the Cinque Terre and the signs of revival are still visible today in the Lombard-style architectural modifications carried out by the Masters Antelami on buildings which, according to various documents, were certainly already established halfway through the previous century. The first mention of the church of S. Antonio di Armesco (Punta Mesco) is in 1380; it is later recorded as a chapel in 1471 and as a monastery in 1618, and definitively abandoned at the end of the 17th century.

54 - The church of Annunziata at Levanto: bas-relief (15ᵗʰ)

16th - 18th century

The raising of buildings and the widening of the urban fabric are evidence of a considerable population increase in these centuries, although accompanied by occasional demographic crises caused by plague and repeated Turkish invasions. In 1545, for example, ten pirate ships sacked Monterosso taking away women and children; raids of this kind were repeated in the first half of the 18th century. Additional work on medieval fortifications and the construction of walls and defence towers like that of Monterosso, or castles like the one on Riomaggiore lent these fortalices the function of refuges during pirate raids, and to fight these invasions lookout shifts were organised at the monastery of S. Antonio del Mesco at the end of the 18th century.

Following the 14th century building and reconstruction work carried out on the main parochial churches and oratories, religious life was enriched in the 16th century by the foundation of various monasteries.

The economy was differentiated: in Portovenere farming, portoro marble quarrying and a small amount of sea trade were well-developed industries; Riomaggiore, Manarola and Corniglia were exclusively farming areas; the activity in Vernazza and Monterosso was equally divided between farming, fishing and sea trade. In Vernazza and Monterosso the growing of mulberries was significant for about two centuries, in connection with the production of raw silk, and subsequently, especially in Monterosso, citrus fruits were also grown (mainly lemons and citrons).

A 1531 census shows a population of 1,983 (but there had been many deaths in Vernazza due to plague), subdivided into 483 family units. In Riomaggiore, Vernazza and Monterosso, each of these units, including servants, consisted of 4-5 people; in the smaller towns of Manarola and Corniglia they consisted of 3, or rarely 4, people. As well as the production of wine, oils and chestnuts for local requirements, wine and even raw silk were exported, and there were little more than 260 head of livestock. Controversies continued between neighbouring authorities over rights to land and goods and the gathering of chestnuts.

In the early 17th century Portovenere had a population of 2,700 and the Cinque Terre 3,000, subdivided into more than 630 family units (Riomaggiore 100, Manarola 80, Corniglia 80, Vernazza 170, Monterosso over 200). The activities of these inhabitants were almost exclusively confined to the cultivation of vineyards on the steeper slopes, and wine production.

In the 18th century a reasonable network of longitudinal and transverse roads existed across the Cinque Terre; their route was generally the same as today's paths and bridle paths. Anyone tempted to think however that the area was not as completely isolated as it is traditionally described to be, should bear in mind that most of the roads could not be crossed by cart, only on foot or by mule. Goods (wine, capers, oil, salted fish, etc.) were mainly transported by sea using "leudi" (heavy vessels) with principal ports in Vernazza and Monterosso.

In 1608 the towns of the Cinque Terre ceased to be autonomous subjects of *podestà* (local authorities) and were annexed to the captaincies of Levanto and La Spezia: Monterosso to the former, and the others to the latter. In 1701 the *podestà* of Riomaggiore/Manarola and Vernazza/Corniglia, with the addition of Volastra, were united as one with the *podestà* administrative centre in Vernazza. The Genoese Republic subjected its territories to monopoly government and fiscal oppression: the inhabitants of the Cinque Terre were obliged to buy wheat, salt and other necessary items on the Genoese market and pay heavy duties on consumption of meat, wine, fish, etc. In 1619 the tunny-fishing nets, a potential source of wealth for Monterosso and existing since the 16th century, were handed over to Genoese aristocrats, who acquired direct control over them as well as over fishing and any other fish trade until 1808. The only compensation offered by the Genoese Republic was a general struggle against pirates which was however short and ineffectual.

19th and 20th century

The end of the Genoese Republic in 1797 signalled the beginning of French occupation of Liguria, which lasted until 1814. The "trees of liberty" were erected also in the towns of the Cinque Terre (and often knocked down) and rosettes were worn, but, like elsewhere, there were protests, uprisings, tyranny and arrests. Considerable difficulties were encountered everywhere due to the re-

55 - View of the 19th castle Umberto I

cruitment of the "armed forces" and payment of levies, also because the beginning of the 19th century with its turbulent politics, occupations and battles gave rise to continual problems in trading farming products, the basis of the Cinque Terre economy. The victory of the reactionaries in 1799, the brief Austrian occupation which imposed heavy taxes, Napoleon's revenge and the return of the French and "patriots", did not however manage to cause any great upset in the Cinque Terre. The Napoleonic wars brought Austrian-English sieges with naval blockades and coastal attacks which also affected Vernazza and Monterosso. The French soldiers protecting the coast left various traces, such as Fontana di Nozzano and some architectural elements of the Casa Boccardi in the Valle di Albana.

At the beginning of the 19th century there was a decisive growth in population and a gradual increase in wine production, which however was never sufficient to guarantee a decent standard of living especially in the eastern-

most towns (Riomaggiore, Manarola) where there was no other source of income.

In 1822 the old Aurelia road, now totally modernised and carriageable, promoted trade which was also facilitated by a renewal in port activity in La Spezia and Genoa. Annexation to the Savoyard kingdom and the consequent rapid industrialisation and militarisation of the Gulf of La Spezia required a city workforce also from the Cinque Terre. The construction of fortifications around the Gulf and on Palmaria, begun in the Napoleonic period, and more general urban expansion led to an increase in quarrying activity and the opening of more quarries (during this period the Ligurian capital was paved with sandstone mainly quarried in the Biassa mountains, known as "Spezia stone").

In the first half of the 19th century a good-sized cargo fleet was formed in Monterosso and Vernazza which soon declined with the advent of steamers and large ships. The economy was still based on farming: cereals, wine, oil, citrus fruits, chestnuts and hay, but also cattle and sheep; along the ridge the mainly oak woods are rich in game, mostly partridge and hare.

The construction of the new Royal Naval Arsenal in 1862, and the railway in 1874, constantly required a workforce and brought the inhabitants of the Cinque Terre closer to different men and cultures. The railway further diminished the local sea traffic and favoured commuting towards the industrial centres of La Spezia and Sestri Levante. In the century after this phenomenon was to become a real exodus, causing many farming areas to be abandoned and wine production to fall.

The farming crisis was particularly accelerated by grape phylloxera, and by excessive subdivision of the land, the continuation of ancient and labourious farming methods, and scarcity or lack of basic facilities. A slight improvement and increase in production has only been noticeable in the last few decades thanks to the use of modern transport techniques (monorails), the development of cooperatives and other factors. Alongside farming activities in importance is tourism, which only developed straight after the war in Monterosso and much later in the other towns.

56 - Vines with low trellis system
57 - "Fasce" with vines

Current socio-economical aspects

The principal farming products are wine grapes and olives for pressing; to a much lesser extent, table grape and olive production, corn, potatoes and vegetables. The already scarce grazing meadows and alternating grassy areas are reduced to a minimal surface area, barely sufficient to feed the few remaining head of mules, horses, sheep, goats and cattle. Above 350m the useful woods are maritime pine woods, the chestnut coppices and, to a lesser extent, oak. Fruit chestnut woods, once quite widespread are now almost totally abandoned and wild.

Vine growing takes place on the terraces, with trellis systems of varying heights between 1 - 2m; at one time vines were grown close to the ground and from the 19th century on low trellises, with the stalks slightly raised about 50cm from the ground, tied with broom to short heather pickets. This labourious system is gradually disappearing and in some areas espalier growing systems (*filari*) have been tested with greater success but sometimes with consequent lower quality and proof. The abandoning of the low trellis vine cultivations is however perhaps inevitable due to the effort and commitment they require. Traditionally the ground must be cleared of grass, the old pickets removed, the ground hoed (with very short-handled two-pronged hoes which allow work to be carried out kneeling down), then replanting of pick-

58 - *The wine cooperative at Groppo*
59 - *A modern monorail*
60 - *In the Cinque Terre women have always made a decisive contribution to agriculture*

ets and the first and second tying, dusting with sulphur (by shaking a bag of sulphur hung on a long, strong cane), spraying with Bordeaux mixture, stripping of leaves and harvesting. Women and elderly folk perform various tasks, but the wearisome transportation during the harvest of the *corbe* (large baskets) full of bunches of grapes is down to the few remaining youths and the

60

stronger men. A significant workforce is required for maintenance of dry-stone walls, paths, water drainage networks and even the typical windbreaking hedges erected with heather branches.

The enormous expenditure of energy and effort required is perhaps one of the primary reasons for abandoning this activity. But this process has recently been halted and in some cases reversed by various factors including: the aforementioned espalier growing methods, the increasingly widespread use of monorails (which are able to carry people and materials on steep slopes with very little effect on the landscape), the experimental use of aircraft to distribute phytochemicals, the creation of a complex water system (which makes use of a spring located almost at sea level, distributing it with a large pump over a wide area), the use of very long-lasting support poles, sowing of leguminous plants to maintain the fertility of the soil, numerous initiatives in support of modern wine production and marketing techniques. This is largely due to the voluntary groups, La Spezia Provincial Agricultural Chairmanship, the *Riviera Spezzina* Mountain Community, the Cinque Terre Park Institution, and the *Agricoltura Cinque Terre* Cooperative.

Between 1913 and 1925 the grape phylloxera destroyed nearly all vines from Corniglia onwards; indispensable at that time was the planting of American vines grafted onto the varieties still grown today, especially *bosco*, *albarola* and *vermentino*. With the exception of a tiny percentage of *moscato*, *regina* and *bosco* grapes sold locally as table fruit,

61 - *An olive grove*

the whole product - 30,000-50,000 quintals (in about 1,000 hectares of vineyards) - is made into wine.

There are four wines which are most celebrated: two are produced in Monterosso, Vernazza, Riomaggiore and the part of La Spezia known as Tramonti up to the council boundary with Portovenere (at Fosse d'Albana) and the other two around Levanto. *Cinque Terre DOC* is a white wine made from grapes from the *bosco*, *albarola* and *vermentino* vines. It is about 11-14° proof with a

62 - *Boats at Monterosso*

dry flavour, a delicate, slightly salty bouquet, a straw yellow colour and is the perfect accompaniment for fish dishes. About 3,200 hectolitres are produced by 270 wine-producing companies, and are qualified according to the vines of origin. *Sciacchetrà DOC* is a highly prized white wine obtained from the same grapes left to dry, the best then being selected. It is a sweet wine of 17-18°, amber or golden in colour. 10 wine-producing companies produce about 79 hectolitres. The rarity and high quality of this wine encourage doctoring, of which one must be careful. Its name, according to some, derives from the local terms *sciaccà* (crush, press) and *trà* (pull away).

Bianco and *Rosso DOC Colline di Levanto* are about 11-13° proof; about 530 hectolitres are produced by 67 companies for the white (Bianco) and 20 for

the red (Rosso).

Olive cultivation takes up about 200 hectares and produces about 500 quintals of oil used almost exclusively *in loco* or sold to nearby traders. The olive groves are often neglected and the land is only rarely cleared of grass, worked and given phytosanitary treatment. More often than not, the olives are simply collected using nets spread under the foliage.

Until about 30 years ago fishing represented an important source of income especially for Monterosso, Vernazza and Portovenere. Rowing or motor boats (*gozzi* or *gozzetti*) were used equipped with long lines and different types of net: the *manata* (an enclosing net, to catch small pelagic fish - anchovies, sardines, etc. - at night with lamps), the *bughea* (a fixed net used for Ox-eyes and other surface fish living near to the shore), the *tremaglio* (for fish near the sea-bed). There are also some trawling luggers of about 15 tonnes each.

The catch is now all sold and consumed locally but until a few decades ago there was a wider market with salting and preserving centres (especially for anchovies) in Monterosso and Palmaria. From the beginning of the 17th century to halfway through the 19th, a tuna fishing net existed in Fegina, near Monterosso, which also represented a considerable source of income and work. Now however the depths have been impoverished from excessive use of trawling nets and proposals have been forwarded for repopulation areas where fishing would be prohibited. Another sea-related activity is mussel-growing, successfully practised in the canal between Portovenere and Palmaria as well as in other parts of the Gulf.

The tourism activity, which began in Portovenere and spread from the beginning of this century to Monterosso, has increasingly involved the other towns in recent decades. The demand for tourism is due to the striking landscape, the artistic and natural merits, the quiet location, the bathing possibilities and the mild climate.

Total hotel capacity offers about 1,000 places, while non-hotel establishments about 10,000. The presence of tourists in hotel accommodation adds up to more than 130,000 per year, principally concentrated between April and September, with peaks in the Easter period and the summer holidays (July-August). More than 25% of current homes in the Cinque Terre are holiday homes. About a million visitors come each year, nearly all in the hottest periods: such a high in-

63 - *Quarrying activity near Levanto*

flux of tourists has caused environmental problems and forced the administration to undertake new projects to raise the quality of services on offer.

The accessible coast for swimming extends for nearly 7km (about 1.5 at Levanto, almost 2 in Monterosso, little more than 1 in Portovenere and 1.5 in Vernazza and Riomaggiore). About 500 boat places are available at the little ports and moorings.

Portoro marble has been quarried in Portovenere since ancient times, but following a long period in which it was developed, it has now been almost completely abandoned both due to exhaustion of material to quarry and also to environmental monitoring. Less prestigious stone quarries are still active on Mt. Castellana while sandstone and serpentine quarries at Monterosso are totally inactive. The Levanto basin represents another important area for quarrying activity: here a particularly beautiful stone is still quarried, although less than before: *Rosso di Levanto*, with its bright variegations of white and red, and other green or very dark breccia of the serpentine group (*Verde di Levanto*) which were used to build columns and various details of churches and other monuments.

Commerce is linked to tourism and is basically represented by a reasonable number of family-run shops. Small craft businesses, also family-run, fulfil the local requirements for woodworking, carpentry, car repairs, building etc..

The human landscape

The Cinque Terre landscape is recognisable by the widespread terraces or *fasce*, which began to be constructed in the 12th century, after a period of Saracen raids. The dry-stone walls, mainly built using blocks of judiciously positioned sandstone, hold back the earth of the terrace above where vines or olives are grown. The good quality and accurate use of the stones, even the smallest and seemingly least important, ensure that the work will last longer, however simple it may seem. Firstly the stones must be prepared, by subdivision according to size and shape, then the foundation, by searching for the most solid points and, if possible, the rock: if necessary this will be smoothed down with a chisel. The wall, whose base is 1-1.5m wide, is erected by first positioning the largest stones perpendicularly to the length of the wall and fixing them with smaller stones. The work then continues with the placing as necessary of more layers of stones, gradually reducing the width of the wall with a slight slope towards the mountain. The gap between the slope and the wall is filled with earth and rubble to ensure good drainage, and finally it is levelled off with earth. Very long, and at times very steep, flights of steps between the terraces have also been built from stone, as well as flat areas to put down and easily retrieve materials carried up by hand, and small steps, little drainage channels alongside the bridle paths, etc. The enormous labour of man over the centuries is clearly evident here on many occasions when the walls, although variable, reach 4-6m in height or have been erected on the coast almost directly on top of the rocks.

It is therefore understandable that farming of this kind was easily abandoned when the traditional isolation of the Cinque Terre came to an end. This desertion and the consequent lack of maintenance have been the major causes of the crumbling of various dry-stone walls, especially those most affected by landsliding. From these circumstances the need arises to search for and motivate a highly-qualified and specialised workforce, along with financial resources to recover these terraces, which are a real monument to man: just think that the total length of the walls adds up to 2,000km! On the *fasce*, the landscape changes during the seasons: in summer, the bright green of the vines prevails or alternates with the light brown of the sandstone walls, in autumn there are the golden bunches of grapes and the red leaves ready to fall, in winter the leafless vines show up the simple but effective architecture of the terraces. Contrarily, the olive groves retain their shiny green and silver tints all year.

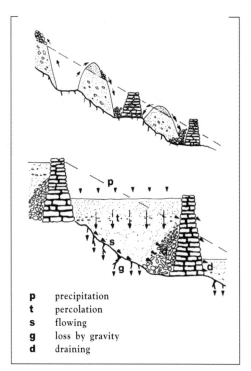

p	precipitation
t	percolation
s	flowing
g	loss by gravity
d	draining

64 - *Earth movement for construction of terraces (top) and the water outflow system (below)*

65 - *The typical landscape with "fasce"*

66 - View of Levanto
67 - S. Andrea
68 - S. Andrea's steeple and the castle

69 - S. Andrea: a detail of the facade

Historical centres and monuments

Levanto

Located at the bottom of a valley nestling in a beautiful bay which is sheltered to the east by the Mesco Promontory. The old centre is surrounded by the walls and contains many works of artistic and historical interest.

Walls and Clock tower

Built in 1265-1271, the walls still protect the old village today.

Church of S. Andrea

In Ligurian Gothic style, with three naves, extended in the 15th century. The facade of white Carrara marble alternating with local serpentine was modified in 1902 and in 1922 two mullioned windows and a rose window were inserted, while above the portal is a 15th century fresco. Inside are two exquisite paintings by Braccesco dated 1493 and other works, among which an Adoration of the Magi by Andrea Semino.

Castle

Of uncertain origins, it was rebuilt in the 14th century, restored several times by the Republic of Genoa and subsequently used as a prison. It has a large round tower.

Medieval loggia

Unique in Liguria for its type and size, this building dates back to 1405; it has a wide portico with four columns in local serpentine, Romanesque capitals, a wooden cover and a fresco from the early 15th century. The magistrates in open court gathered here.

Church and convent of the Annunciation

Built in 1449 and rebuilt in 1615, it was restored in 1981. There is a frescoed open gallery and inside, paintings by Pier Francesco Sacchi (early 16th century), Bernardo Strozzi and Giovanni Battista Casoni (17th century).

Poor Clares Convent

Built between 1605 and 1688, it now houses the civic offices, the *Carabinieri* station and other offices. It has a large courtyard and a church dedicated to St Rocco.

Church of S. Maria della Costa

Of ancient origins but rebuilt in 1334 and restored in 1719; the baroque facade still shows some original elements.

S. Giacomo Oratory

Consecrated in 1600.

70 - Medieval Loggia
71 - Medieval Loggia: a detail of the recently restored 15th fresco
72 - The village of Monterosso from the "castle"

Restani House

Old seat of the Town Council and Captaincy, once on the seafront. Large 13th century ogival arches.

Permanent crafts and traditions exhibition
A museum specialising mainly in rural traditions and crafts; includes a library specialising in ethnography and dialects.

Monterosso al Mare

Typical valley-bottom coastal centre spread over two small inlets, sheltered to the west by the Mesco promontory. Composed of the old village, whose historical centre is mostly intact, and the modern town of Fegina. According to some sources, it is of Roman origin, but the oldest fortified nucleus built on the hill of St. Christopher began to fulfil an important defensive role in the 7th century during the Longobard invasion.

Church of S. Giovanni Battista
Parish church of 1244 in Ligurian Gothic style, with three naves: two-colour facade with tracery rose-window, ogival portal, lunette with fresco (baptism of Christ); baroque interior. Crenellated steeple, erected in 15th century by raising a pre-existent watchtower.

Capuchin monastery
Built in 17th century and houses precious paintings including works by Luca Cambiaso, Bernardo Castello, Bernardo Strozzi, and an exquisite crucifixion incorrectly attributed to Van Dyck.

Oratory of Morte ed Orazione
Baroque in origin, contains a statue of St Anthony Abbot from the monastery of Punta Mesco, now in ruins.

S. Croce Oratory
16th century.

73 - *The tower steeple of S. Giovanni Battista*
74 - *S. Giovanni Battista: a view of the facade*

75 - Vernazza from the sea

Ruins of castle and walls
Impressive ruins of medieval *castrum* are incorporated into the current cemetery on the Colle di S. Cristoforo.
Aurora tower
Built in 16th century as defence against pirate raids.
Neptune or Statue of Giant
Reinforced concrete sculpture, 1910, by Arrigo Minerbi of Ferrara.

Vernazza
Typical tower-shaped houses extend along a river valley and rise up on the summit of a rocky outcrop, which hides the view of the centre to anyone approaching from the sea. Steep and narrow alleyways descend to the main street and the little square on the natural harbour where more complex architecture is to be found, like loggias, porticoes and decorated portals. Until 1000 the population was mainly centred on the hills of Reggio.
Church of S. Margherita di Antiochia
Built in Ligurian Gothic style by the Masters Antelami, it has undergone repairs and extensions. Three naves and an octagonal steeple 40 metres high.
Monastery of Reformed Franciscan Friars Minor
Built in 17th century, includes a turret and ancient walls which are probably from a previous period.
Belforte towers and castle
Remains of pre-11th century fortifica-

tions; include ramparts on the sea and two round towers, one of which is situated behind the centre, on the path to Corniglia.

Corniglia *(part of the municipality of Vernazza)*

Only coastal village of the Cinque Terre to be built not on the seafront but on a promontory about 100m high, steep and inaccessible from the sea. Towards the mountain the town opens onto a natural and intensively cultivated basin which has determined its rural characteristics.

Church of S. Pietro

Splendid Ligurian Gothic-style construction of 1334, built over a chapel dated pre-1000; three naves, facade with white marble tracery rose window (by Matteo and Pietro da Campiglio), round arched portal and lunette enclosing small sculptures; inside, a 12th century baptismal font.

Old post house

Building with Gothic arches in black stone traditionally known as the old post house of the Fieschi.

Remains of the Genoese fortifications

Remains of a castle and a 16th century polygon tower are incorporated in the cemetery over the sea.

Oratory of the Flagellants of S. Caterina

Manarola *(part of the municipality of Riomaggiore)*

12th century village partly perched on an outcrop and partly extending along a natural canal, the Rio Groppo, now covered. The most important historical buildings are concentrated in a pretty square in a commanding position.

76 - *Corniglia: church of S. Pietro*
77 - *Manarola: church of S. Lorenzo*

78 - *Riomaggiore*
79 - *Riomaggiore: church of S. Giovanni Battista*

Church of S. Lorenzo, or of the Birth of the Virgin Mary, and steeple
Basilica with three naves, built in 1338 probably by the Masters Antelami; it has a Gothic facade with marble tracery rose window and a portal with lunette on top, on which a bas-relief portrays the martyrdom of St Lawrence. The interior, with baroque modifications, has a valuable 15th century triptych. The square-based 14th century steeple faces the main body of the church.
Flagellants' Oratory
14th century building.

Riomaggiore
The centre, reportedly dating back to the 7th century, has tower-shaped houses arranged along the narrow Rio Major valley parallel to the stream (now covered), with steep flights of steps and alleyways furrowing vertically through them. A "fishing quarter" faces the sea and a "farming quarter" the mountain.
Church of S. Giovanni Battista
Basilica with three naves and square apse, built in 1340. The facade was renovated

last century and has early Romanesque elements (bestiary figures, basket capitals, etc.) which pre-date the construction of the church. The interior is divided by elegant ogival arches, and contains a large wooden crucifix by Antonio Maria Maragliano, a painting attributed to Domenico Fiasella, other exquisite 17th and 18th century paintings and a mechanical organ dated 1851.

Flagellants' Oratory or Church dell'Assunta
15th century building with valuable triptych showing the Virgin, Child and Saints John the Baptist and Dominic.

Castle ruins
Begun in 1260 by the Marquesses Turcotti di Ripalta and completed by the Republic of Genoa, it has two round towers and wall ruins incorporated subsequently into a cemetery.

Chapel of S. Rocco and S. Sebastiano
Built in 1480 in commemoration of a plague; beautiful triptych inside.

Portovenere and surrounding area

A maritime depot of Roman origin with a terrace of "tower-houses" ranged on the Doria quay making a village-fortress, built by the Genoese republic in the 12th century and unique in Liguria. Opposite are the islands of Palmaria and Tino.

Church of S. Pietro
Built over an ancient Roman temple, it has palaeo-Christian (4th-5th century),

81 - *Interior of S. Pietro*
82 - *S. Lorenzo*
83 - *S. Pietro's steeple*

proto-Romanesque, Romanesque and Gothic (13th century) elements, with Nola' style tower.

Church of S. Lorenzo

Built by the Genoese in 1116 to the Masters Antelami's design, it underwent modifications until the end of the 16th century. It has three naves, a Gothic transept and Renaissance presbytery, and a facade with elegant ogival doorway. Inside are works by the Sansovino school, Mino da Fiesole and Bernini. Also of interest are a log of Lebanese cedar which washed up on the beach in 1204, and 15th century effigies of the white Madonna, venerated due to avoided outbreaks of plague and famine in 1399.

Church of S. Lorenzo Parish Museum

The museum contains one Byzantine and three Syrian caskets from the 11th century and Ligurian-Tuscan triptychs from the 15th and 16th centuries.

Fortified castle

This was begun in 1161 and completed in the 16th century.

Castrum vetus

Original location of the settlement, now identified by a flat area surrounded by ruins of the walls which connect the village to the church of S. Pietro.

Gate, walls and tower

The Genoese began construction of the walls in the 12th century and they surround the town to the west linking it to the castle. The gate is characteristic with an 1113 inscription and rustic work tower

with two and three mullioned windows.

Church of S. Maria of Le Grazie and former Olivetan convent

The sanctuary built in the 15th century in the Le Grazie district is late Gothic in shape; inside is an exquisite wooden choir with altarpieces attributed to G.B.Casone and D. Fiasella. Alongside the church are the ruins of the cloister, while in the adjoining, former Olivetan order convent is a fresco by Nicolò Corso (16th century, restored).

Roman villa of Varignano

The ruins of this country residence date to the 2nd or 1st century BC, but cover a period up until the 6th century AD.

They include a heating system, a cistern, an antiquarium with marble statues, ceramic remains and large containers for grain.

Ruins of the abbey of St. Venerio

Situated on the island of Tino the restored ruins of a church and Romanesque cloister dating back to the 11th century are all that remains of an abbey abandoned in 1400 after repeated pirate raids.

Ruins of the Tinetto hermitage

The remains of a small church with two naves and a coenoby dating back to the 5th century are situated here on the cliffs of Tinetto.

84   - *The bay of Le Grazie*
85   - *Le Grazie*

ITINERARIES

The islands

The Island of Tino

The charm of a trip to Tino, the ancient Tyrus major, lies in the particular nature of each island environment, the strict access restrictions and its natural and historical merits.

The island is a military zone, now only accessible on the occasion of the St. Venerio festivities around the 13th September. For a single day, boats and ferries provide a direct link between Tino and Portovenere and La Spezia; however it is necessary to stay well-informed right up until the moment of departure, as the sea conditions may oblige the authorities to make changes in the programme. From the mooring at the north-eastern point of the island, moving west, the remains of the 11th century monastery can be visited, of which the facade and splendid early Romanesque cloister have recently been restored. The St. Venerio Coenoby was founded around 1056, probably on the ruins of an older church built on the tomb of the saint, who came here from Palmaria to live as a recluse, and it acquired great importance in the late Middle Ages when it became the proprietor of the three islands and other lands. The

86 - The island of Tino

importance of the monastery diminished in the 15th century due to Saracen raids, which forced the monks to withdraw into the Le Grazie bay; it ceased altogether at the beginning of the 19th century when Napoleon arrived.

A few metres from the sea is a narrow natural cave, 11 metres long, which is home to rare cave insects. The north-western coast bears evidence of the ancient portoro quarries, and a white lighthouse tower stands over the island.

Sailing around Tino provides an opportunity to admire the luxuriant vegetation of a mixed holm oak and Aleppo pine wood which, over about 200 years, has replaced older plantations; to the south a white sheer cliff is bordered with scented rosemary plants. On the rocks isolated clumps of the Portovenere corn-flower grow alongside festoons of rock samphire (which can be observed more closely near the mooring). A little further west large tree-spurges can be seen. Yellow-legged gulls and other sea-birds nest on the cliffs; the island fauna is enriched by the presence of the leaf-fingered gecko, a real living fossil which often occupies the dry-stone walls, ready to hide away in the cracks.

To the south the islet of Tinetto rises from the sea which is little more than a simple rocky crag but has important historical evidence: Byzantine monks arrived here around the 6th century bringing holy relics to safety from the advancing Vandals and Arabs. At that time the two islands were possibly still joined together and the monastery, later destroyed by the Saracens, was built by the Byzantines on a jutting spur, like today's church of St. Peter in

87 - *The Aleppo pine and holm oak wood on the island of Tino*

Portovenere. The ruins of Tinetto consist of a tiny oratory with apse and a chapel with two naves and oratory attached, and cells from a later period. Leaf-fingered gecko and lizards (possibly of an exclusive breed) scurry about between the stones and tangled bushes of the islet.

 ## The Island of Palmaria

The island can easily be reached from La Spezia or Portovenere by regular ferries (in the summer period) or by boat, and there is an easy path running around the perimeter. Here there are interesting sights such as imposing 19th century fortifications, disused portoro quarries, interesting features of Mediterranean vegetation, many caves, plant species exclusive to the area and rare birds nesting on the high, sheer cliffs. The island's name probably derives from the term *Barma* or *Balma* (cave) and not from the age-old presence of the palmetto, although this hypothesis

The rock roses of Palmaria belong to three different species: the Montpelier rock-rose (Cistus monspeliensis) with small white flowers and dark, sticky, wrinkled leaves; the sage-leaved rock-rose (Cistus salvifolius), with large white flowers and light-coloured leaves, downy underneath; and red rock-rose (Cistus incanus), with its large red flowers and leaves edged with felt. The first two are common all over the Riviera and on almost all Italian coasts, while the third is quite rare in Liguria and confined to isolated places. Palmaria is the only place on the eastern Riviera where red rock-rose can be seen.

88 - Red rock-rose

should not be completely discarded.

Men have come to the island since prehistory, and from the 6th to the 11th century it was the site of an important monastery dedicated to St John the Baptist. Subsequently the life of the monks was concentrated on the island of Tino. Along with Portovenere the Genoese Republic made it a defence stronghold for its eastern borders. Militarisation of the island reached a peak during the Savoyard rule with the construction of imposing fortifications which acted as lookouts over the highly important mouth of the Gulf of La Spezia. The many caves, maquis landscape and beautiful cliffs increase its touristic interest.

Route:	a
Altitudes:	departure: 0
	arrival: 0
	maximum: 175
Sum of height differences:	530
Length:	6.5km
Difficulty:	slight
Time:	2¹/² hours

After disembarking at the Terrizzo moor-ing, follow Via Schenello towards the east, almost as far as the 19th century castle "Umberto I", once used as a prison, which is situated on the Scuola (or Scola) point opposite which, on the sea, is the quadrangular Scuola Tower, a fortification built by the Genoese in the 16th century.

Just before the castle turn right onto a track, which leads, on flat ground, to the pretty Cala della Fornace among sweet-smelling Spanish broom, rock-roses with bright blooms, myrtle with its delicate scent and other maquis plants.

The road leads on to Punta della Mariella where it forks into two: the first proceeds on the left towards a tunnel where it ends, and the other rises on the right to 95m in altitude. Follow this latter path, but if you wish to stay on level ground it is possible to link up with it by zig-zagging up the ridge of the Punta della Mariella. Go down the south-eastern slopes among old terraces now colonised with Spanish broom and vine-tie, a species which prefers periodic fires and stony, well-aired, limestone soil. You arrive at the Cala del Pozzale at the camping village reserved for air force per-

89 - *The western coast of Palmaria: the island of Tino in the background*

sonnel; a landing stage is located here for the ferries to La Spezia, Lerici and Portovenere operating in the hours of greatest use during summer. Portoro quarries can be seen here, which were active until a few years ago, and *Rhaetavicula contorta* limestone (from a little more than 190 million years ago) on the upper part of the island covering the solid dolomitized limestone which is more recent (less than 190 million years ago) but is now situated underneath due to overturning phenomena.

Continue towards Punta Ziguella and then begin to go uphill again; turn right ignoring the path on the left which leads to Capo dell'Isola where quarrying activity has left imposing signs. To the south the island of Tino can be seen, with its white lighthouse tower standing out in the dark green of the woods. The path passes about 30m above the Grotta dei Colombi which has provided scholars with abundant human and animal remains, probably neolithic. The entrance is about 32m in altitude and is accessible only with the help of a rope, from a small path branching off to the left. Other caves can be found all along the south-western coast of the island between sea-level and the summit.

The path rises again, offering a splendid view of the waves breaking on the high cliffs frequented by birds requiring isolated habitats: pallid swifts, red-rumped swallow, blue rock thrush, yellow-legged gulls, rare shag. Between the cracks in the rocks the exclusive Portovenere cornflower blooms. The path crosses formations dominated by holm oak, vine-tie, Spanish broom, tree spurge and other bushes. Below in the Cala Grande are six caves, into one of which flows one of the island's very rare natural springs.

We reach the top of Palmaria between Forte Cavour on the right and the semaphore telegraph construction on the left; ignore the tarmacked road and proceed along a short-cut to the left, which is at first gently sloping but later very steep. The descent leads through Aleppo and maritime pines, passing high above the Grotta Azzurra, accessible by boat, and reaches the north-western point of the island at a niche which once housed the bust of King Carlo Alberto in honour of his visit to the quarries in August 1837. Beyond the narrow inlet, the tiny church of St. Peter seems almost tied by a fine umbilical cord to Portovenere on the background of the imposing limestone walls of Muzzerone.

After circling round the Carlo Alberto quarry, like a wide grotto with the vault supported by a central pillar, continue along the northern coast passing near an old kiln and Villa S. Giovanni, possibly the site of the ancient monastery of St. John the Baptist. Bordering on the naval bathing facilities, the path returns to the starting point, in the Seno del Terrizzo, from where the north slope of Palmaria can be seen, occupied by a cool gully with chestnuts, pubescent oak and other species, in strong contrast with the rest of the vegetation which is clearly more thermophilous.

90 - *The western coast of Palmaria*

The long excursions (longitudinal paths)

The Ridge Route:

 Portovenere - Punta Mesco - Levanto

Route no.	1
Altitudes:	departure: 5
	arrival: 2
	maximum: 780
Height differences:	2977 (+1487, -1490)
Length:	33.6km
Difficulty:	slight
Time:	13 hours

A long trip, tiring but not hard, which ascends onto the ridge and along it among woods and open spaces, overlooking the whole Cinque Terre landscape from on high. The last section can be varied, with the same travelling time, by descending to Monterosso instead of Levanto; also the route can be interrupted at various points using tranverse links to coastal towns. To better understand the itinerary and facilitate use of the guide, the description has been divided into 4 sections, but the ridge can also be crossed in shorter sections.

91 - The paths on the coast and halfway up the slopes are the most frequently used

 Portovenere - Campiglia

Route no.	1
Altitudes:	departure: 5
	arrival: 400
Height differences:	525 (+460, -65)
Length:	4.8 km
Difficulty:	slight
Time:	2¹ᐟ⁴ hours

As well as the opportunity to observe interesting species of flora and fauna, the first leg of the ridge itinerary, steep and rather tiring initially but easy in general, offers some of the most beautiful views in the Riviera. It is possible to join paths 11, 4b and 4a, which descend to the sea or to La Spezia, and at the destination refreshments are available in the form of a drinking fountain and *trattorie*.

The route begins from the piazza (bus terminal) to the right of the medieval town gate where *Colonia Januensis 1113* is still legible, and ascends steeply with high irregular steps cut into the rocks, between acanthus plants and wall pellitory. Alongside the castle walls the path becomes less steep and crosses the maquis, which has prevailed over the abandoned olive groves. On the left is the little church of St. Peter, jutting over the sea, and the island of Palmaria; on the right are the waters of the Gulf of La Spezia.

On the western slope large cushions of tree-spurge and the rarer wild olive are combed by the wind: their presence indicates warmer and dryer climactic characteristics than on the rest of the eastern Riviera. The path ascends steeply again to Mandrachia or the Cava Canese; on the left a small diversion takes us to a splendid and scenic terrace: the Aleppo pines frame the backdrop of the sea and the white vertical cliffs rise sheer more than 100m above the rocks and foaming waves. In spring the Portovenere cornflowers stand out on the rocks, exclusive plants to this promontory and the islands in front of it, while the pretty, ancient Apuan globe daisy is rarer and indigenous to the Apuan Alps and the Tuscan-Emilian Apennines. Great care should always be taken here and children held firmly by the hand to prevent them from nearing the edge of the precipices.

The main path with route 1 turns right almost on level ground on the slopes facing the Gulf of La Spezia until it fuses with the tarmacked Muzzerone road, which must be followed downhill through a wood of maritime pines, pubescent oak and hornbeam as far as the Sella Derbi. It is also possible to go uphill almost as far as the 19th century Muzzerone Fort with the variant 1a, with its splendid blooms of rocket candytuft, Canterbury bells, sword lily and various orchid species, but also unforgettable glimpses over the craggy coast high above the sea, with vertiginous precipices reaching 350m, framed with small holm oaks and ancient, small Aleppo pines. Lovers of birdwatching can lie in wait here to observe the flights of red-legged partridge, ravens, blue rock thrush, red-rumped swallow and even peregrine falcon. Around the fort is a rock climbing training site, pleasantly situated facing the sea, which allows enthusiasts to practice their skill. On reaching the Fort go down to the Sella Derbi and rejoin the main route.

From this mountain saddle, at the memorial tablet for aviators fallen in 1937, the path ascends the slopes of Mt. Castellana (496m) through extensive maquis, sometimes dominated by rock roses and sometimes by tree heath or holm oak. A small jutting "terrace" offers a splendid scenic view towards Portovenere and Palmaria; from here a difficult path leads off through the maquis slightly downhill to a private building shaped like a castle. The area we are now crossing shows contact lines between different geological formations acting as intermediaries between the limestone *Lama della Spezia* and the sandstone *Macigno*: alternating over a very small space are flinty limestone (180-175 m.y.a.), Posidonomya marls (175-160 m.y.a.), jasper (160-135 m.y.a.), majolica (135-100 m.y.a.), and polychrome shales, evidence of a longer period (100-26 m.y.a.). Thus the countryside acquires a particularly pleasant variety of colours: yellowish grey, burgundy, dark grey, grey-green or rosy white blend together, also due to the structural movements which at times fold, squeeze and roll the subvertical layers of rock.

The path passes high on the Valle d'Albana, dominated by a large holm oak wood (sadly damaged by a violent fire in the winter of 1987) and emerges on a bend of the tarmacked road leading up from La Spezia to Campiglia.

Follow this for a few metres and the path takes up again on the left crossing a beautiful pine wood with holm oak and maquis undergrowth. The road is reached again more or less where path 11a branches off to the left towards the sea at the bottom of the Valle d'Albana. Passing a few houses and a small playing field, it then re-enters a pine wood; at an altitude of about 400m there is a small path on the left which is worth the brief diversion to a beautifully scenic spot on the coast, where the view extends from the Tinetto rocks to the east to the Ferale rocks opposite Schiara to the west. The main path encounters the stone tower of an old windmill, perhaps from 1840, used in the past for grinding chestnuts, and continues alongside the church of St. Catherine to reach, at last the small square of Campiglia.

92 - The rocks near Muzzerone

Campiglia - Colle del Telegrafo

Route no.	*1*
Altitudes:	*departure: 400*
	arrival: 513
	maximum: 570
Height differences:	*263 (+188, -75)*
Length:	*3.2 km*
Difficulty:	*slight*
Time:	*1 hour*

This section of the ridge route continues from the previous one, also number 1, through a semi-natural landscape. It sets off from the medieval village of Campiglia, which can be reached from Portovenere and from La Spezia by road, bus or on foot from Acquasanta with path 11.

A flight of steps leads up from the fountain, near the main square, and crosses the ridge with beautiful views over the whole Gulf and, in the distance, the Apuan Alps: some of the higher peaks soar up (Sagro, Pisanino, Pizzo d'Uccello) and the marble quarries whiten the mountains like snowy capes. Between terraces both cultivated and abandoned, the route reaches Casa Lardon, surrounded by pines, and at the next fork turn right entering a pine wood, damaged by fires. Continue for a short, even section and you reach a bend in the carriageable forestry road leading up from Campiglia to the Telegrafo. The route continues upwards through the pine wood, along the ridge of Rocca degli Storti, staying slightly to the west side.

It then follows the carriageable road, for a section along the slopes facing the Gulf and then those overlooking the open sea, and the sharp contrast can be observed between the cooler, damper woods of chestnut and the other deciduous broadleaf trees (manna ash, hop-hornbeam, pubescent oak) on the inner slopes, and the comparatively dryer evergreen maritime pine and holm oak woods with maquis on the outer slopes. This situation is linked to differences in microclimate and earth, partly however caused by man's diffusion of pines and chestnut trees. Small examples of cork oak may be encountered on the west-facing slopes at a height of 570m, one of the highest stations in Liguria for this species.

The remaining section crosses a widely used area which can easily be reached by car from La Spezia; here it is possible to exercise in the majestic green pine wood

93 - Group of cork oaks

94 - *Campiglia*

using the equipped exercise route, or sit in the picnic areas with tables and benches. The forestry road reaches the chapel of S. Antonio whose apse offers a small shelter in bad weather. Paths 4 and 4a join us here, which descend steeply towards the sea at Schiara, Monesteroli and Fossola, and on the other side, towards Biassa.

It is interesting to note the strong presence under the majestic maritime pines of holm oak and maquis bushes like tree heath and arbutus, almost forming a second forest under the conifer wood; if fires and other action could be avoided, the broadleaf forest would soon prevail. Two very similar rubiaceous species close together, but with completely different ecological requirements, can be observed:

the oval bedstraw, a species found in the western Mediterranean and north-west African coastal area, preferring cork and holm oak woods, and the round-leafed bedstraw typically found in beech or other deciduous woods of the Eurasian mountains. After a very slight ascent the path leaves the road to follow the ridge among pines, chestnut and maquis, and finally arrives, in slight descent, at the Colle del Telegrafo and once again on the forestry road. Here there are *trattorie* and a car park, and the tarmacked road heading from Biassa and La Spezia to Mt. Verrugoli, Mt. Parodi and La Foce. This is an important crossroads which indicates the beginning of the *via dei Santuari* and the destination of route 3 from Riomaggiore.

Colle del Telegrafo - Colla di Gritta - Punta Mesco

Route no.	1
Altitudes:	departure: 513
	arrival: 324
	maximum: 780
Height differences:	1787 (+799, -988)
Length:	20.8 km
Difficulty:	slight
Time:	8 hours

95 - Mt Verrugoli

This long section touches the summits of the mountains surrounding and protecting the Cinque Terre; it reaches scenic points and crosses various vegetational features. Unlike the other routes, the effects of human activity on the area are less evident and there are almost no vine or olive terraces, but instead woods and copses of bushes. The Colle del Telegrafo can be reached from Portovenere and Campiglia by route 1 itself, or from Riomaggiore with routes 3 or 3a, or by car on the La Spezia - Biassa - Mt- Parodi road, or again using the *via dei Santuari*. The many intersecting paths encountered provide opportunities to break up the route and link up to the towns on the coast or in Val di Vara.

To the right of the *via dei Santuari* the path ascends steeply almost to the ridge among the Mediterranean maquis, damaged by fires, but with conspicuous flowering of orchids and mountain cornflowers, up until a few feet from the Bramapane or Verrugoli Fort; to the west the Cinque Terre appear lined up on the sea as far as Mesco. At the Bramapane fork, a track leads left to Casella in Val di Vara, while to the right it joins up immediately with the tarmacked Colle del Telegrafo - Mt.

Parodi road and two uphill paths, for Mt. Verrugoli and Fort Bramapane. Follow the unmade road around Mt. Verrugoli (745m), crowded with aerials, and along the ridge to Sella La Croce, ignoring route 4e which goes down to Biassa. Ignore too route 01, which leads from Sella La Croce down to Riomaggiore and on the left, Carpena and La Foce.

Having left the road which continues down to the right, the path continues slightly uphill just under the ridge of Mt. Galera. From here the Canale Ruffinale (or Rio Finale) can be seen with a large viaduct over it, and, on the sea, Manarola. A little further on at a group of large chestnut and pine trees, medieval Carpena can be seen and the slopes leading from La Foce and Mt. Parodi down to the Vara, an extremely interesting area with extensive karst phenomena (sinkholes, *sprugole*, potholes, furrowed fields) and fossils, especially ammonite, but also an important strategic transit point between the Gulf of La Spezia and Val di Vara. Continue along the sea-facing slopes in a mixed wood of turkey oak, chestnut and pubescent oak; as well as Manarola, Volastra now appears on a natural terrace. You will come across a small shelter dug out during the last war, which is useful in case of rain, and just after this, route 02 which links Manarola to S. Benedetto. The route now follows the ridge of Mt. Capri in a chestnut and turkey oak wood; a few metres from the path on the right is a *menhir*: two blocks of oblong-conical stone which formed a single piece more than three metres high now nestle among a tangle of ferns and brambles.

The path continues just under the ridge, on the sea-facing slope, in a sparse wood with abundant bracken and rock-roses. The Montenero sanctuary, Manarola, Volastra and Groppo are all visible below. On arriving at the saddle between Mt. Capri and Mt. Cuna, branch off to the right, avoiding the ridge of Mt. Cuna, on the mountain facing slope where St. John's Lily, mountain cornflower, small meadow rue and, in autumn, heather flower among the large lichen-encrusted boulders. Our route now enters, on level ground, a chestnut and hop-hornbeam wood, mixed here and there with hazel and aspen. The knotty cranesbill, tormentil and bladderseed indicate respectively a cool, submountainous environment and the presence of north-western floral elements. Among the branches the pretty S. Gottardo chapel can be glimpsed in a coppice of holm oak and holly. The route quickly reaches the north-west saddle of Mt. Cuna and descends steeply along the ridge in a mixed wood of maritime pine and broadleaf trees, with a thick undergrowth of broom and bracken; after crossing the Rio Molinello it arrives at the south-east saddle of Mt. Marvede. Here it encounters route 6 which links Manarola and Casella; this saddle

forms the entrance to a wide depression, with vegetation damaged by fires and cutting, which ends up in another little saddle from which route 5 leads off to S. Benedetto in Val di Vara.

The route continues on level ground among pines and then descends slightly in a beautiful oak wood with thorny undergrowth of gorse, tree heath, brambles and bracken; it then crosses the southern slopes of Mt. Marvede in a large shrubby formations of holm oak which survived the fires and the invasion of gorse. The ridge of Mt. Marvede also shows a clear contrast between heat-loving holm oak vegetation on one side, and cool environments on the other with chestnuts and hop-hornbeam. On the left are visible first Case Porciano and then Corniglia, while in the background the Mesco Promontory appears. At the saddle north-west of Mt. Marvede, where there is a wide, green glade with pines and holm oak, the route joins path 7a which ascends to Corniglia, and passes route 7 which links Vernazza to Riccò del Golfo.

Now the route ascends the slopes of Gaginara until it encounters the unmade road from Fornacchi. On Gaginara too there are some of the most extensive gorse and holm oak shrubberies in Liguria. Continuing slightly uphill and then almost levelly it circles round the peak of Gaginara on the sea-facing slope, where thick banks of sandstone can be seen; the view of Punta del Mesco and Monterosso al Mare is magnificent. The cooler microclimate is here confirmed by the presence of a chestnut wood with hop-hornbeam, manna ash, hazel and a rich undergrowth of reed bunting, red heather, knotty cranesbill, mountain cornflower, black salsify-leaved rampion, Piedmontese wood-rush, peach-leaved bells.

Having proceeded around the Gaginara, we reach another saddle from which a path branches off across Mt. Baudara to Riccò del Golfo; we continue, however, up the ridge of Mt. Castello through a sparse pine and chestnut wood, and then on follow on level ground, a narrow path sometimes hidden by ferns; below, Vernazza and its towers appear. Entering a thick copse of chestnut we encounter a ruin which acts as a trigonometric sign-post, 5,360m as the crow flies from Mt. Verrugoli. The next long section is slightly downhill, firstly on the sea-facing slope and the ridge, and then on the mountain side in a splendid chestnut wood, and then again facing the sea until the clearing called Prato di Corvara, where we join route 05, an ancient path leading to the old village of Corvara. Ascending again the slopes of Mt. Malpertuso, the highest mountain in the Cinque Terre (815m), the settlement of S. Bernardino is visible low down on the left. Just after this is a steep descent, through chestnut, pine and holm oak, arriving at a wide unmade road. The bends can be cut across with short cuts to reach Casa Tartarelli. Should you miss the last short cut, you rejoin the path shortly in any case by continuing along the road which passes near Case Rossi.

The route crosses Foce di Drignana, a saddle where the council road passes to link Vernazza to Pignone in the Val di Vara, and then continues up to a gentle ridge; by turning left here onto the tarmacked road you would reach the

Reggio Sanctuary and Vernazza along route 8. However we continue straight on, slightly uphill, in thick holm oak and gorse vegetation to the Carpilè saddle. Continuing to the right for a short distance, remaining on the mountain slope instead of ascending Mt. S. Croce, we reach a second saddle known as Sella Schisarola. Near a power line we encounter two paths: one coming from Mt. S. Croce which we have just circumvented and the other which leads down on the left to the *via dei Santuari* and on the right towards Case Gagge. We continue straight on amid thick gorse vegetation which interrupts the maritime pine and chestnut woods, occasionally victims of fires, as far as Termine on the provincial road connecting Monterosso and Pignone. Here the *via dei Santuari* and route 8b for the Reggio Sanctuary both begin. Go down the tarmacked road on the left and after about 1.5 km you will reach the sanctuary of Madonna di Soviore, from which bridle path 9 branches off to Monterosso. On the opposite side, another road known as Alta Via delle

96 - *The Vernazza valley*

97 - Case Drignana

Cinque Terre leads to Poggio (on the ridge forming a boundary of the valley amphitheatre of Levanto) and much further north-west to Mt. Zatta where it joins the Alta Via dei Monti Liguri (a trekking route which follows the whole main crest of the alpine and Apennine chain in the region). Descending for about 2km along the tarmacked road as far as Colla di Gritta, we encounter the coastal Levanto-Monterosso road. From here it is possible to reach Levanto directly avoiding Punta Mesco and cutting out 5km, by following route 12 which passes through the small locality of Fontona. Instead we continue uphill to the left of the Hotel/Restaurant on a small path with two little bends, across a thick pine wood

and then in a mixed wood of holm oak, chestnut and pine. Under the trees, scorpion senna, hairy greenweed and bright pink everlasting pea bloom; here and there, in the sunnier clearings there are garrigue features with spiny spurge and serpentine plantain, especially where serpentine and gabbro rocks emerge. Beyond Mt. Molinelli, which we pass on the side facing the Levanto basin, we ascend again on Mt. Rossini; on the right we can see Chiesanuova, Legnaro and other small communities belonging to Levanto, while behind us is the Sanctuary of Soviore which we have recently left behind. Almost at the summit of Mt. Rossini, there is a superb view from a rocky spur of the bay of old Monterosso and the Punta Mesco; we go down and then up again on the Montenegro (which can be recognised by the presence of a telegraph relay station) with its steep eroded slopes, colonised by Salzmann's greenweed and a few pine trees. Descending again we reach the Sella di Mt. Vè, or Colla dei Bagari, where various paths cross: 14 and 14a, going uphill from Levanto and Monterosso respectively to the summit of Mt. Vè, and 22 going down to Levanto across the Costa di Sopramare. In this saddle an interesting vegetational formation can be observed, with plants more or less exclusively linked to ophiolitic substrata: Salzmann's greenweed, with cushions of stiff, almost prickly branches, the beautiful native Ligurian lavender cotton, Ligurian spiny spurge, with typical semi-circular cushions, Nice spurge with its upwards-pointing branches. These are accompanied by other plants native to poor, dry terrain such as wild carnation, thyme, cantabrian bindweed and mountain germander. Here, as on almost all the ridge between Colla di Gritta and Punta del Mesco, numerous butterflies can be seen: Cleopatra, brimstone, painted lady, red admiral, woodland grayling, etc.

We pass over a stream and continue, almost on level ground, on the eastern slopes of Mt. Vè; just underneath is Casa Bagari, now abandoned, and on the sea the bay of Fegina. Here and there grow small pubescent oak and blue Canterbury bells bloom. We continue along the ridge among heather, bracken, rock roses and tree heath (with some groups of individuals more than 3m high); along the path, note the stratigraphical contact points between the Gottero sandstone and older Palombini shales. The path goes gently downhill into a pinewood as far as a fork, which can easily by identified by the octagonal stone tower. Route 10 crosses here, going left to Monterosso, while route 1 turns sharply right towards Levanto. Before continuing down it is worth making a short diversion of about 200m towards the point of the promontory: this

is a magnificently scenic spot with a view of all the Ligurian Riviera, from Tino to the east as far as the Maritime Alps in the west. On a particularly clear day you might glimpse the Tuscan islands and Corsica. On the point, before the precipice, are the ruins of the monastery of S. Antonio.

98 - The route n. 1 near Soviore

99 - Noteworthy plant communities on the serpentines near Montenegro above Monterosso
100 - Punta Mesco from the "Monterosso castle"

 Punta Mesco - Levanto

Route no.	1
Altitudes:	departure: 324
	arrival: 2
	maximum: 324
Height differences:	402 (+40, -362)
Length:	4.8 km
Difficulty:	slight
Time:	1¹⁄⁴ hours

This route enables you to reach Levanto in a short time, and is usually well-used in both directions as a connection between Monterosso and Levanto. Because the station at Levanto is served by more trains, excursions to Punta Mesco often begin in Levanto and follow the first part of route 1 in the opposite direction to that described below. Along the route is a great deal of important historical evidence and there are many beautiful scenic glimpses.

From the fork above the ruins of S. Antonio, the route leads slightly downhill on a convenient bridle path on the sea-facing slope of Mt. Vè. There are extensive and magnificent Mediterranean shrub formations here, with tree-spurge, majestic arbutus and heathers over 4m high with trunks 50cm in diameter (once intensively used for briar pipes). A beautiful, intricate holm oak wood extends along a valley as far as the sea, while light Aleppo pines cling on the steeper coast where gulls and peregrine falcon fly overhead. Among the vineyards we encounter first Casa Lovara, then Casa Nuova and finally Case S. Carlo, and draw closer to the cliffs: jutting over the sea are the Scoglio Nero, Punta Spiaggia and Punta La Gatta, where excellent sandstone was once quarried. A bronze memorial plate recalls the tragic death of Wilhelm Maier, professor of Physics at the University of Freiburg, on 25th April 1964. On reach-

101 - Punta Mesco: the revived maquis after the fires

ing the tarmacked road near the restaurant "La Giada", proceed for about 500m and then take the path on the left which descends steeply to Levanto among olive groves, vines and pretty houses. A marble slab recalls how on the terrace of Casa Massola, known as the "casa rossa", Guglielmo Marconi carried out experiments in radio connection between Levanto and S. Margherita Ligure in 1930-1.

Finally we reach the little piazza of Levanto's medieval castle, from where a flight of steps lead to the promenade near the Casino.

The Blue Route (coastal route):

 Riomaggiore - Monterosso

Route no.	2
Altitudes:	departure: 8
	arrival: 5
	maximum: 220
Height differences:	987 (+492, -495)
Length:	11 km
Difficulty:	slight-fairly
Time:	5 hours

This is the most classic Cinque Terre excursion, because it visits the five seafaring towns and crosses coastal environments in a framework of intermingling sea-and sky-blues and the bright colours of the maquis. Whether you prefer to pause at the picnic areas outside the towns, or taste the delicious dishes and prestigious wines in the centres themselves, the villages must be visited. The route can be broken up by using rail or maritime links or by taking up intersecting paths. The first section, between Riomaggiore and Manarola, is a splendid walk along the waves, known as *Via dell'Amore*. The route can easily be broken up into stages: Riomaggiore - Manarola (1km, 20 min.); Manarola - Corniglia (3km, 1 hour); Corniglia - Vernazza (4km, 1 hour and 40 min.); Vernazza - Monterosso (4km, 2 hours).

102 - "Via dell'Amore"

From the station of Riomaggiore, a flight of steps leads us to the famous *Via dell'Amore*, carved out of the rock a few metres from the sea between 1926-28 during the initial stage of doubling of the railway line, and it has recently been restored. Previously the only route from Riomaggiore to Manarola was by sea or by the *Via Beccara*, which led up and then down again on the Costa di Corniolo. The Via dell'Amore is even and properly paved; there are plenty of benches to rest on. The rocks house plants well-suited to the salinity: rock samphire, wild cliff carrot, maritime cineraria, sea purslane, Queen's stock and slightly higher up hardy examples of tree-spurge. Exotic agaves prevail over pittosporum and prickly pear. The view opens over the whole Cinque Terre coast. Above a few abandoned vineyards have been invaded by maquis; on the rocks and steeper, barer slopes the Luni cornflower and golden eternal flowers bloom, while in the gentler areas holm oak takes root. The imposing layers of sandstone forming the Tuscan Macigno can be admired, with their imprints of waves and currents left millions of years ago. These are the banded sandstones of Riomaggiore, with their characteristic feature of alternate light (sandstone) and dark (argillaceous shales) bands, and sometimes showing enormous folds.

Opposite, on a black spur, the houses of Manarola can be seen. In a small basin surrounded by crags, the struggle takes place between the very narrow strips of vineyards and the natural vegetation characterised by tree-spurge and other elements of maquis. The route passes alongside the railway and down to the station of

103 - Manarola

Manarola, and through a pedestrian tunnel to the town.

Continue toward the sea along the main street, which constitutes the covering of the Rio Groppa, between two multicoloured terraces of houses and the boats pulled up onto dry land and "parked" under the houses. On reaching the mooring, continue on the seafront along an ideal extension of the Via dell'Amore, built in 1968. Behind, the houses of Manarola are almost miraculously positioned on top of each other on the vertical cliffs. We pass around Punta Buonfiglio and reach a second mooring, older than the former; here the convenient paved surface ends and we begin to go uphill along a path where Queen's stock and cineraria grow alongside fig trees and vines, left over from former plantations. A shrine to the Virgin Mary built in 1860 is placed at the crossroads with a path edged with pretty caper and rosemary plants leading up among the vines to Volastra. The cultivated vineyards give way to extensive maquis of tree-spurge which rest during the summer and give an ever-changing multicoloured effect (from light green to red and then paler and paler yellow until the leaves fall).

The route takes us about 30m above the shingle beach of Corniglia, on a small path threatened by landslides. Opposite, Corniglia looms over the rocky precipice of Punta del Luogo; here we can observe the contact points between banded Riomaggiore sandstones and the dark

104 - *Corniglia's train station and the long pebbly beach*

shales of the Canetolo Complex, a large knee bend and a white limestone inclusion. Various small paths lead down to the sea but they are often closed or difficult to pass. Some of the spurges reach a height of 3m, which is exceptional for Liguria. Prickly ivy (*Smilax aspera*) and spiny asparagus are entangled on the abandoned vines. We encounter a few small houses and cross two gullies subject to landslides; the substratum, clearly shaly, belongs to the argillaceous schists of the Canetolo complex. Small cultivated vines alternate with tree-spurge formations, garrigue and rocky vegetation: thyme, red spur-valerian and golden eternal flowers grow abundantly here.

When we arrive on the top of a railway tunnel, now disused, we must descend towards its opening where a cool spring gushes forth. Flowing the old railway track across the Rio di Valle Asciutta and the Villaggio Europa, a long row of bungalows, we then turn right under the railway bridge which crosses Rio Molinello and arrive at the station.

The route continues along a wide walkway alongside the tracks and up 33 convenient flights of steps to Corniglia; here we can see the wide basin behind the station, like a mosaic of vines and maquis, framed with a pine wood and strips of holm oak wood, the group of houses at Porciana and further east, some of the houses of Volastra. Landslides noted in ancient times fed the beach below and forced the rail-

105 - Vines and olives between Corniglia and Vernazza

activities have been carried out to defend the railway line which until the 1960s ran along the foot of the landfall. Above on a precipice is the village of S. Bernardino. We continue up through the olive groves to the pretty houses of Prevo, and here meet a brach off the right which leads up to S. Bernardino; we go down again and on the left a very scenic route enters the village near a spring and the rejoins our own path. The olive groves are behind us now, replaced by maquis of terebinth trees, tree heath, spiny broom and holm oak; here and there in the grassy areas blue millet, cock's foot, quacking grass and wild fennel grow. We cross the landslide area of Macereto and Vernazza appears with its two towers, while on the right a path goes

way route to be moved into the tunnel, and imposing walls to be built.

At the top of the steps, we continue along a lane to a little fountain, where route 7a branches off up to Cigoletta, and alongside the parish church of S. Pietro: the present building dates back to 1334 but has undergone various interior renovations; the Gothic facade has a tracery rose window from 1351. From here we can go down into a little piazza to visit the town, and then follow the tarmacked road linking Corniglia to S. Bernardino.

From the road we go down towards a beautiful stone arch bridge over the turbulent waters of the Groppa, and follow a bridle path among olive trees as far as a fork where we go down to the left towards another small bridge; the path to the right leads to case Fornacchi (7b). We now go uphill again, still among olive groves, ignoring several paths on the left which lead to Punta Tre Croci and Gùvano beach, wedged into one of the most beautiful bays of the Cinque Terre.

We transversally cross the landslide area of Gùvano: strengthening and draining

106 - View of the Mesco

street of the town, which covers a stream. Vernazza is certainly worth seeing, before going up again through an alley (via Ettore Vernazza) between the houses and later the vineyards; on the left the little harbour can be seen and the pretty church of S. Margherita di Antiochia, in gothic-Ligurian style, dating back to 1318, with a 40m belltower.

Cross the small bridge over the Fosso Vignaresca and go up steeply among the vines, which are crossed by monorails. This modern method of transport has in recent years facilitated the task of the landworkers, leading to renewed wine-production activity.

The route, now less steep, crosses olive groves and reaches a natural rocky terrace above Punta Linà, offering a remarkable scenic glimpse of Monterosso and Punta

107 - Church of S. Margherita d'Antiochia
108 - The coast near Punta Linà

uphill to S. Bernardino and continues as far as Cigoletta and Casella, in Val di Vara (7b).

Here prickly pears grow extensively alongside tree-spurge and agaves; a large crag reveals wide surfaces of banded sandstone layers. On the horizon, the Mesco promontory shows up the contact points between the Gottero sandstone on the front of the promontory, and the Palombini shales of the early Cretaceous period towards the ground. Here we encounter a tower entirely covered with ivy; on the sea lower down the "Belforte" rises up with its round tower. We now descend steeply along little lanes and steps between houses tightly heaped together as far as the main

Mesco. The maquis, dominated by holm oak, is beautiful here, and here and there large rocks and arid areas emerge where cineraria and antirrhinum, which its large sulphur-coloured blooms, flower. After short, alternating uphill and downhill sections through crops now conquered by the maquis, we cross Costa Mesorano as far as the little bridge over Fosso di Crovarla, and a spring. We cross Fosso Mulinaro and the Valle Acquapendente canal on an arched bridge; the name of the canal ("hanging water") derives from the fact that its copious waters gush into the sea in a magnificent waterfall. Straight after Casa Acquapendente the path narrows and circles on level ground round a ridge covered in vines, and a steep flight of

109 - *The path between Vernazza and Monterosso*
110 - *Monterosso al mare (on the sea): an appropriate name*

steps leads down along a ditch to the back of the Porto Roca hotel. From high up Monterosso seems divided into the old village with the 13th century church of S. Giovanni Battista, and the more recent settlement of Fegina. On arriving in Piazza Garibaldi we continue past Torre Aurora on the seafront where the station is situated and where route 10 begins.

Via dei Santuari

 Colle del Telegrafo - Sanctuary of N.S. di Soviore

Altitudes:	departure: 513
	arrival: 542
	maximum: 545
Height differences: 703 (+366, -337)	
Length:	25km
Difficulty:	slight
Time:	7 hours (on foot)

This is a route halfway up the coastline which can be followed on foot, on horseback and by mountain-bike, but also by car. The route encounters, or in some cases passes close to, five sanctuaries, one for each maritime village. To the east the route joins the Colle del Telegrafo crossroads. From the parvises of the sanctuaries and here and there along the route there are superb views. This route is of religious and also historical interest because it visits what were the original Cinque Terre more than a thousand years ago, small peasant villages overlooking the sea from a certain distance. The sea is an important element both as a backdrop and for the extraordinary collection of offerings it has inspired. The road forms a frame for the Cinque Terre, acting as a separation between the widely cultivated lower area and the almost completely wooded upper region. It crosses several vertical paths and it is preferable to follow it entirely by bicycle, or on foot, although in this case just visiting one or two sanctuaries each time or completing the routes. There are no particular problems involved in finding the route because it is consistently wide and often tarmacked; for this reason no detailed description seems necessary but a few points should be emphasised.

From the Colle del Telegrafo, the road initially joins route 3a at the foot of Fort Bramapane, above the old Case di Lemmen and then zigzags downhill along the ridge of the Rocca dei Pini, alongside the houses of Cericò, mentioned in 1251 for swearing loyalty to the Genoese Republic in the war against Pisa.

Route 3a branches off to the left and down on a path to the Montenero Sanctuary, while the road, after a few bends, enters the Riomaggiore Gorge. It follows the western slopes of Mt. Verrugoli and the eastern slopes of Mt. Grosso as far as the Costa di Campione, where it meets route

The first certain mention of the Sanctuary of Nostra Signora di Montenero dates back to 1335, but it is traditionally held to have been already present in the 8th century. Its present appearance derives from renovations in 1847. Inside, a 16th century painting has replaced a much older image of the Virgin, now lost, traditionally connected with miraculous events, including the welling up of a precious spring.

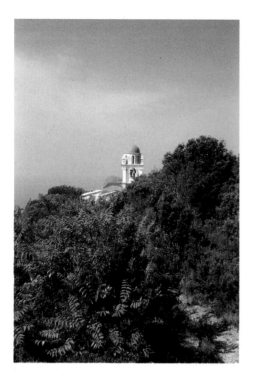

111 - N. S. di Montenero
112 - N. S. della Salute at Volastra

01 heading from Riomaggiore to Sella La Croce and Carpena.

The road continues, almost level, along the Rio Finale (Canale Ruffinale) valley; on the Costa di Corniolo to the left route 02 ascends from Manarola towards the saddle south-west of Mt. Galera. It enters the Groppo Canal valley, passes the Fosso di Crovo and Tavola and Pizzoli Streams, then leaves the wood to go downhill to Volastra, meeting up with the east and western branches of route 6 between Manarola and Mt. Marvede and then the coastal road between Volastra and Manarola.

From Volastra to Porciano, or the Pianca houses, it is possible to choose as a variation route 6d which passes almost parallel, just below the road, first through vines and then in the maquis and in a pine wood. It branches off from the small square in front of the church at an iron cross set in an old

The sanctuary of *Nostra Signora della Salute* at Volastra shows clear Romanesque influence and dates back to the 10th century. The decorations under the roof, a Gothic mullioned window and the ogival sandstone portal stand out on the simple facade. The interior, which has been altered several times, contains a splendid triptych on gold-backed canvas from the 14th century depicting St Lawrence, to whom the church was originally dedicated, with St Dominic and St John the Baptist. Volastra ("Land of Olives") was perhaps a post house for changing mules and the houses are arranged in characteristic concentric semi-circles on an originally marine terrace.

stone seat. The road itself continues for about 5km reaching a height of around 500m, with wide views over the Cinque Terre coast. The monorails can be observed at close range; these modern and fast means of transport for people and materials are highly suitable for the rough structure of the Cinque Terre. The road reaches Porciana: a few houses and a tiny chapel whose origins are claimed to be Roman; above the road is an experimental vineyard. Beyond the Rio Molinello, which forms the boundary between the municipalities of Riomaggiore and Vernazza, we encounter Case Pianca and Barani on the left among the cultivated land. Here route 7a joins us from Corniglia and follows the road for about 300m, and then continues uphill through the holm oaks just before Fosso della Groppa. The road reaches Case Fornacchi where there are glimpses over Corniglia, S. Bernardino and Prevo, over the landslide area and

113 - S. Bernardino

the beach of Gùvano. We also come across routes 7b (Zuara-Corniglia) and 7 (Vernazza- Cigoletta). On entering the Vernazza gorge the tarmacked road branches off to the left to descend to S. Bernardino and from there to Vernazza or Corniglia.

The sanctuary of Nostra Signora delle Grazie at S. Bernardino was built at the beginning of the 19th century to replace a pre-1584 chapel traditionally held to have been founded by the Sienese saint while preaching in this area. The church towers up on a ridge where a small village has developed and which overlooks the impressive Guvano landslide.

The *Via dei Santuari* continues on almost level ground through the gorge, which is much cooler than other areas of the Cinque Terre: here chestnut woods, hop-hornbeam, pubescent oak, turkey oak and hazel are at their most extensive. In the undergrowth mesophilous plants flourish such as knotty cranesbill, black salsify-leaved rampion, wood-rush, hairy greenweed, and wood melick. On the better exposed and sunnier ridges, on the other hand, are holm oak or mixed woods (chestnut and holm oak, or chestnut and maritime pine), but especially on the ridges, pine woods which are ruined to a greater or lesser extent or shrubby areas with gorse. After a few kilometres we come across route 8c, ascending from Vernazzola to Case Montagù and the ridge, and we follow the boundary between the Case Borella farmland and a beautiful holm oak wood where, in the undergrowth, the rare oval bedstraw grows. On reaching Drignana,

an important crossroads, the route crosses route 8, on its way up from Vernazza, and the Vernazza- Pignone road; higher up at the pass, route 1 passes by following the main ridge of the Cinque Terre. Route 8 is worth following downhill for a few metres as far as the Reggio Sanctuary, amongst majestic trees. The area between Foce di Drignana and Reggio is sprinkled with houses, most of which are inhabited, which once made up ancient nuclei from which the population then moved away to found or enlarge the more important towns

The sanctuary of Nostra Signora di Reggio is built on an ancient burial and worship site near the nucleus which formed the origins of Vernazza. Mentioned in 1248, it was built in the 11th century over a large crypt (now inaccessible) and renovated in the 14th century. The facade has a gable with atypical decorations. The church, slim belltower, lodge and hostels make up a complex which is not only visited for veneration of the image of the Virgin, legendarily attributed to St Luke, but also for a rest in the shade of majestic trees, enjoying the scenic view over Vernazza.

of Vernazza and Pignone.

Taking up the route again, we now reach Case Pearino and, among the maquis, which has been burned by fires several times, Termine, where route 8b from Reggio, route 1 following the ridge to the right, and the important provincial Colle di Gritta-Pignone road meet up. The *Via dei Santuari* ends here, but it is worth following the route for another 1$^{1/2}$ km along the provincial road as far as the Soviore Sanctuary, from which you can quickly go down to Monterosso on route 9.

114 - N. S. di Reggio
115 - N. S. di Soviore

Soviore is probably the original nucleus of Monterosso and was already established at the time of the invasion by the Longobard king Rotari. The sanctuary of Nostra Signora di Soviore was mentioned in 1225, but the present building has been repeatedly restored and altered. It has a beautiful 14th century portal with marble bas-relief and inside a wooden statue of the Pietà dated at 15th century. The steeple has mullioned windows and crenels decorated with ancient white marble columns and capitals. The impressive adjacent lodge, begun in the 18th century, along with the parvis completes this complex in which the layering of different renovative styles over time can be observed. This is the most frequently visited sanctuary in the Cinque Terre thanks to its lodgings and restaurant, its position on one of the main communication routes and its magnificent views of Monterosso, Mesco and even the Alps on a clear day.

Vertical routes

From Riomaggiore

Riomaggiore - Colle del Telegrafo (via Lemmen)

Route no.	3
Altitudes:	*departure: 8*
	arrival:513 (maximum)
Height differences:	*505 (ascent)*
Length:	*4.5 km*
Difficulty:	*slight*
Time:	*1 3/4 hour*

Along this highly scenic route one can visit small Medieval settlements, reach an important crossroads linking the Cinque Terre to the Gulf of La Spezia and complete long excursion routes of about 40km, including blue route 2 along the coast, ridge route 1 or the *Via dei Santuari* route passing halfway up the coast. At the destination a pleasant rest in a trattoria awaits. Taking the pedestrian tunnel from the station we reach the east part of the village and follow the length of the main street, which constitutes the covering of a watercourse. We then turn along a convenient bridle path and on up through the Valle dei Mulini, with the watercourse sometimes on our right and sometimes on our left, crossing first farmland and then entering the cool green vegetation. After the old mill, avoid the diversion to the left which arrives at the aqueduct springs and instead cross the coast road, encountering after a short distance a pretty stone bridge and the distinctive entrance of a farmstead, with its gate and three niches. The route turns to the right, continuing uphill through pines, chestnut trees and farmland; Mt. Verrugoli can be seen high up, bristling with aerials. In the cool valley which we now follow, several rare ferns can be seen like the Tyrrhenian fern, lanceolate spleenworth, Madeira fern. The route leads to the grassy parvis of the Sanctuary of S. Maria di Montenero, an ancient complex of buildings which have been rebuilt many times (p. 101). The portico can shelter several people in case of rain; from the benches in the shade one can admire the view of Palmaria, Tino and Tinetto, and the coast as far as Mesco to the west.

Go up a few steps and continue uphill, on the Montenero coast which is one of the most scenic points of the Cinque Terre. Then turn sharply right, up a few more steps to Casarino; from here we will cross

116 - Boats at Riomaggiore

the little valley of Serra, mostly on even ground through vines flat on the ground and innumerable dry-stone walls, to reach the houses at Lemmen. These are older than the maritime village of Riomaggiore, and according to some writers, their name derives from ancient Greek civilisation. Their existence was mentioned as far back as 1200, in connection with a route halfway up the coast joining the settlements of Lemmen, Cericò, Casarino and Montenero, all called to swear loyalty to the Genoese Republic in 1251 against the Pisans. Next to the stone houses are a pretty chapel, a trough carved by hand out of the rocks and a cableway, where a branch of the route leads down to the tarmacked coast road. Turning left, the route continues steeply uphill where crops give way to natural vegetation and encounters an artificial cave dug by the Germans in the last War, and just after, at Crocetta, a small wooden cross. It then turns right, where the ascent is less steep and after a short distance reaches Colle del Telegrafo.

117 - An old cableway near Lemmen

the old houses of Cericò.

We follow the main road (Via Don Minzoni) for a few metres, which consists of the covering of the Riomaggiore stream, and then turn abruptly right up a flight of steps scrambling between the houses. Turn left again into Via Libertà and after a few metres on level ground take a long flight of steps up to the left through vineyards to the provincial road, which you must cross. The route passes round the cemetery and uphill again still through vineyards, with a splendid view over

 Riomaggiore - Colle del Telegrafo (via Cericò)

Route no.	3a
Altitudes:	departure: 8
	arrival: 513
	maximum: 515
Height differences:	509 (+507, -2)
Length:	3.8 km
Difficulty:	slight
Time:	1 hour and 35 minutes

This is a scenic variation of route 3 and the first section is steep and tiring. The route passes the Montenero Sanctuary and

118 - The dominant location of the Montenero sanctuary

Riomaggiore, Punta del Mesco in the distance on the sea, and to the east the precipices of Capo di Montenero.

When you reach the junction between the provincial Riomaggiore road and the state highway of the Cinque Terre, follow the latter for about 250m. You then pass round the Capo di Montenero ridge for a wider view to the east over small coves and craggy promontories. Above the road a small flight of steps leads through vineyards again, some abandoned and overrun with tree heath. We continue briefly uphill and turn to the left; here we continue on level ground and then uphill again towards the Montenero coast ridge: now the view opens up to included the islands of Palmaria and Tino, edged with white limestone cliffs. To the west Manarola, Volastra and further still Monterosso can be seen.

We reach the Sanctuary of Montenero, with its baroque features restored in the 19th century (p. 101), and join route 3 for a short section. We go up a few steps and pick up the route again, remaining on the crest, in the maquis of heather and gorse, to arrive at Casarino; here we leave route 3 to proceed straight uphill into a mixed woods of chestnuts and pines. After a short distance we reach the *Via dei Santuari*; we follow the hairpin bends among strips of holm oak wood as far as the houses of Cericò on the slopes of Mt. Verrugoli. When the ascent is at an end we turn right leaving the wood and after few hundred metres we arrive at the Telegrafo, an important intersection of routes.

 Riomaggiore - La Croce

Route no. 01

Altitudes:	departure: 8
	arrival: 637 (maximum)
Height differences:	629 (ascent)
Length:	2.8 km
Difficulty:	fairly
Time:	1³/⁴ hour

This a steep uphill route directly reaching the ridge of the Cinque Terre (route 1) and continuing beyond the crest towards the ancient village of Carpena; here there are ample scenic glimpses of the whole of the Cinque Terre.

From the imposing 13th century castle of Riomaggiore we go up a flight of steps onto a very steep path through the vineyards, with views over the houses of Riomaggiore and the white Montenero Sanctuary. At 175m we join the coastal state highway and after a few metres west we take another flight of steps up to the path following the ridge of the Costa di Campione. The route passes an ancient shrine and just after this enters a sparse pine and chestnut wood where it reaches the *Via dei Santuari*, crosses it and continues uphill with views over the Montenero Sanctuary, Fort Bramapane and Mt. Verrugoli. The path now becomes a conveniently paved bridle path and after two small hairpin bends we reach Sella La Croce, along with a convenient unmade road linking Casella (in Val di Vara) and the Bramapane intersection, and route 1. At this point, then, we can either return following other routes downhill towards the Telegrafo and Riomaggiore, or continue with route 01 toward the ancient villages of Carpena and Castè, as far as La Foce.

From Manarola

Manarola - Mt. Galera

Route no.	01
Altitudes:	departure: 20
	arrival: 708 (maximum)
Height differences:	688 (ascent)
Length:	3.4 km
Difficulty:	fairly
Time:	2 hours

This is a scenic route with views over extensive terraces of vineyards and olive groves, and is also interesting from a naturalistic point of view due to the variety of woods it crosses; from this route we can join ridge route 1, and after a few hundred metres see a *menhir*, or continue towards S. Benedetto in Val di Vara.

We begin by following the main street (Via Roma) which covers the Groppa Stream, with the option of a short cut through an alley on the right between the houses which reaches the small square in front of the 14th century church of S. Lorenzo.

119 - Ruins of Riomaggiore castle
120 - Manarola

The first section of the route follows the stream between vegetable gardens and dry-stone walls; we then go up a flight of steps overhung with rocks on which golden eternal flowers, spur-valerian and Balbis's pink stand out. The paved path crosses more vegetable gardens and vineyards, sometimes enclosed by walls. On the opposite slope we can see Volastra high up.

The route continues parallel to the road to Volastra and after a short distance joins it, where the variation to the west (via Volastra) of route 6 branches off for Mt. Marvede. Immediately on the other side is a shrine with a small spring and a little stone bridge across the Groppa Stream: the variation east of route 6 (via Groppo) branches off on the left.

We scramble up uneven stone steps to 325m high, through mainly low trellis vines, on strips of land a few metres wide; higher up, many of these have been abandoned to the grass and maquis bushes. At the bottom of the valley we can see the village of Groppo, with Volastra above it, its houses arranged in a semi-circle among the olives on a terrace formation resulting from erosion by the sea or, more probably,

the presence of faults and sliding of blocks of stone. Just under a house we turn to the left on the level and enter a pine wood; we go uphill a short way, encountering here and there large rocks covered with carpets of moss, and reach the ridge of the Costa di Corniolo, along which a wide path runs. Immediately on the left, almost on level ground, is the *Via dei Santuari* and beyond it a small path leading towards the crest, where beautiful St. John's lilies flower. There is a view over Volastra, Manarola and the Montenero Sanctuary.

121 - Groppo

In a small dip we continue on the level, to the left, through a wood consisting of pines, chestnut trees, pubescent and holm oak and manna ash, among marguerites, and Seguier's pinks. This leads us gradually into a shady chestnut wood with species preferring cooler conditions such as black salsify-leaved rampion, wood-rush, knotty cranesbill, and yellow pimpernel. At about 540m high at Fosso Crora edged with alder trees, you can drink at the Corvo spring; we then continue uphill, sometimes steeply, into a mixed wood of pubescent and turkey oak. The route now meets route 6b which reaches our own destination but leaves from Manarola and passes through Case Bovera on the Volastra slope. Turning abruptly right we continue with route 6b and after about 200m we meet route 1: the saddle of Mt. Galera is a little further ahead on the left. At this point we can continue on the ridge towards Sella La Croce or Mt. Marvede, to see the *menhir*, or else enter the Val di Vara to reach S. Benedetto.

 Manarola - south-east saddle of Mt. Marvede (via Volastra)

Route no.	6
Altitudes:	departure: 20
	arrival: 667 (maximum)
Height differences:	647 (ascent)
Length:	3.7 km
Difficulty:	slight-fairly
Time:	2¼ hours

This route has urbanistic, architectural and natural points of interest and has several variations, one of which (6d) visits the village of Volastra, the original centre of Manarola, with its Romanesque 10th century church of Nostra Signora della Salute, and also the cellars of the Cooperative Agricola Cinque Terre at Groppo. The route then continues towards Casella in Val di Vara . Difficulties may arise at times from vegetation impeding progress on foot. The first part of the route is identical to the previous one, and therefore no description is necessary here. From the crossroads dividing route 6 and route 02, we continue along the tarmacked road but almost immediately go up a gentle flight of steps through olive groves, as far as the settlement of Volastra.

The houses of this village may be Roman in origin (Volastra = *Vicus oleaster* = land of olives), and formed a mule changing station. However the only remaining original feature is the arrangement of the houses in concentric semi-circles, suited to the structure of the terrace on which they are situated, and a few houses rest only on two adjoining rooms. Slightly to one side is the Romanesque church of N.S. della Salute, originally 10th century (p. 102), opposite which route 6d begins towards Case Pianca. We however must go straight uphill along the *via dei Santuari*, and after the bend pick up a path on the left between dry-stone walls surrounding olive trees. At the fork, we go slightly uphill to the right and encounter vineyards, and a hut with a cellar, an excellent position to observe the urban structure of Volastra from above. We then turn sharply left (the path to the right comes from Groppo), walking first through vines and then along an embanked path, often overrun with thorny gorse.

We now arrive at the Case Bovera, which are mainly abandoned and reduced to ruins. To the right route 6b branches off in the scrub, on its way to the north-west saddle of Mt. Galera. After a short, almost flat section, among chestnuts and pines, the route follows uphill a very steeply embanked path, sometimes almost hidden and made impenetrable by gorse, whose growth is favoured by fires.

The difficulties come to an end after about 400m, when we reach a section where the wood appears to be better-preserved; we go uphill through a strip of holm oak wood

122 - *Volastra*
123 - *Mules resting near Cigoletta*

encountering open areas with scented Spanish broom. Here precipitous crags can be seen to which ancient holm oaks cling and we cross many streams flowing into the Fosso Molinello. After 250m, first on flat ground and then slightly uphill, through a mixed wood of turkey and holm oak, manna ash and chestnut, we reach the south-east saddle of Mt. Marvede, where we also meet ridge route 1. The latter leads away on the left towards Cigoletta (15 minutes) and upwards on the right to Mt. Galera, in the direction

111

of Portovenere. If we continue straight on, crossing the saddle in a backwood of poplar, turkey oak and brambles we arrive at Casella, in Val di Vara.

From Corniglia

Corniglia - Passo della Cigoletta (via Case Pianca)

Route no.	7a
Altitudes:	departure: 100
	arrival: 612 (maximum)
Height differences:	512 (ascent)
Length:	2.8km
Difficulty:	slight
Time:	1 hour and 40 minutes

This route offers scenic glimpses and observation of the frequent contrasts between the maquis and vineyards; it also intersects various other routes.

From the centre of Corniglia behind the gothic parish church of S. Pietro, the route turns uphill between vines and dry-stone walls, on an initially easy paved path, with low steps here and there. The vines are grown at various heights above the soil and in the most exposed places hedges of dry heather branches protect them. The path, sometimes easy and sometimes steep, passes through abandoned vineyards and farmlands overrun by the maquis.

There are scenic glimpses of Monterosso and Punta Mesco, jutting out into the sea; on a nearer crest S. Bernardino can be seen, threatened by a landslide below. After a hairpin bend the path, almost always straight and easy, continues through olive groves (mostly abandoned) on the eastern

124 - Corniglia

125 - Corniglia and the eastern coast from S. Bernardino

slope of the Fosso della Groppa valley. On the opposite slope the contact point can be seen between pine woods and vineyards; in the cooler and shadier areas, there are also pubescent oak, chestnut and cherry. Continuing uphill the olive groves are completely overrun by spontaneous vegetation, including some gorse bushes. This species is predominantly distributed in the Atlantic areas of Europe and limited in the Cinque Terre to higher altitudes on cooler slopes; fires almost always favour its growth. The path enters a pinewood with traces of terracing and on the right path 6d begins, which leads halfway up the coast to Porciano and Volastra. We however must continue upwards in the pine wood passing near Case Pianca to reach the *Via dei Santuari*. We follow this to the left and after the first bend to the right we pick up a path which leads uphill in the pine, holm oak and chestnut wood. We cross a shrubby area of heather, broom, gorse and bracken, with attractive blooms of Seguier's pink and St. John's lily, to reach ridge route 1 in a clearing; we then continue on flat ground for about 400m amidst a sparse pine wood with an intense undergrowth dominated by gorse, heather and bracken, as far as Cigoletta. Here one can continue along the crest (route 1) or down into the Val di Vara towards Riccò del Golfo (route 7), return to the sea at Vernazza (route 7) or back to Corniglia via Fornacchi (route 7 and 7b).

 Corniglia - Zuara - Cigoletta

Route no.	*7b*
Altitudes:	*departure: 100*
	arrival: 612
Height differences:	*512 (ascent)*
Length:	*2.4 km*
Difficulty:	*slight-fairly*
Time:	*1¹/² hours*

This route gives a scenic view of the Guvano landslide and the villages surrounding it; confused signposting and steepness however make it difficult and tiring. At the destination is an important intersection with other routes.

The first section, from the station at Corniglia, is the same as "blue route" 2; after the bridge on the Fosso della Groppa, and before the second, take the path on the right among the olive trees. The grass under the trees is embellished with dozens of different flowers; love-in-a-mist, red pimpernel, borage, ophrys, and orchids. After crossing Fosso Canaletto we reach the S. Bernardino-Corniglia road and continue on an old bridle path among the partly abandoned olive groves.

The route leads almost to the edge of the old landslide and up to the right on a small, very steep path among vines and strips of maquis which have overrun the "fasce". The houses of S. Bernardino overlook the precipice below which the beach of Gùvano is situated. The maquis has completely replaced the vines and Spanish broom, spiny broom, tree heath, and holm oak bloom here, with pretty Luni cornflower between the stones.

Cross the *Via dei Santuari* and go up again steeply to a vineyard; proceed alongside the Case Fornacchi and you arrive at a plateau with vegetable gardens and meadows, once used to produce fodder for mules and the other few head of cattle. Here we join route 7, going up from Vernazza, on the cart path and continue on, firstly slightly uphill and then almost on flat ground as far as Cigoletta where we meet ridge route 1.

113

From Vernazza

Vernazza - S. Bernardino - Cigoletta

Route no.	7
Altitudes:	departure: 10
	arrival: 612
	maximum: 667
Height differences:	688 (+648, -40)
Length:	3.7 km
Difficulty:	slight
Time:	$1^{1/2}$ hours

This route is the same as route 2 at the beginning and offers remarkable views over Vernazza and the rest of the Cinque Terre, as well as the opportunity to observe obvious contrasts between the extensive landslide movement and intense terrace shaping carried out by man; there are also plenty of historical and architectural points of interest. The route can join up with other paths or continue to Riccò del Golfo in Val di Vara. Follow the main street (Via Roma), which forms the covering for the Vernazza stream, for about a hundred metres then turn left into Via M. Carattino and follow route 2 uphill through the houses and then along a flight of steps surrounded by rocks and dry-stone walls with cineraria, tree-spurge, Balbis's pink, *Grattalingue* (*Reichardia picroides*), rue and spur-valerian. At a circular stone tower covered with ivy the village can be admired from above, stretching out along the gorge and the rocky spur carved by the waves, with Belforte above, also with tower. The banded sandstones arranged in almost vertical layers show clearly the alternation of a coarse, light arenaceous

126 - Vernazza
127 - A rustic wine-cellar near Vernazza
128 - View of Vernazza

component and a finer, pelitic, dark grey one. In the distance beyond Monterosso, the Punta Mesco shows on the other hand the contact points between the front, consisting of Gottero sandstone and the rear part of Palombini shales. We encounter vegetable plots and vines, a reservoir and a large crag with banks of banded sandstone. On the rocks the Luni cornflower and rue grow abundantly, while the surrounding area is dominated by tree-spurge and naturalised exotic species like agaves and prickly pear.

We turn left, leaving route 2 which continues on to Corniglia, and take up route 7 which leads around a ridge and uphill between dry-stone walls, vines and abandoned terraces. Opposite on the other slope, we can see route 8 (Vernazza - Reggio Sanctuary), the Franciscan friars minor monastery and part of the town walls. We follow a crest running parallel to the coast among the maquis, with heather, tree-spurge, myrtle, terebinth, holm oak and spiny broom, and abandoned vineyards, and steeply uphill with small hairpin bends. The view alternates between the landslide area of Macereto to the east and Punta Mesco to the west. Vineyards and vegetable plots overlap and a cableway and more modern monorail can be seen close up. The route emerges near a house on a flat and shady lane: on the left the Vernazza valley is enclosed by the ridge with Mt. Malpertuso (the highest in the Cinque Terre). We now take up a path to the right, among vegetable plots, vines and fields until we reach Sella di Comenecco, where we cross the tarmacked Corniglia - S. Bernardino - Vernazza road and, after a short distance to the left we go uphill to the right, arriving at a house, and then continue on the northern slope on flat ground. Gorse is seen only on this cooler slope, which emphasises its Atlantic nature and the fact that it requires a high level of humidity, and also shows the microclimactic contrast deriving from the difference in exposure within a few metres. At a hut we turn right on flat ground among vegetable plots and vines, instead of downhill to the left.

This leads us to the houses of S. Bernardino, arranged along the ridge separating the Vernazza valley from the Fosso Canaletto and the spur of Corniglia; in the village, set in a saddle, is a church built at the beginning of the 19th century, possibly on the ruins of an older chapel: there is a drinking fountain at this point (p.103).

The route continues in front of the church, leading alongside a house and up into a pine and chestnut wood. Reaching a crest we can see Manarola, Corniglia, Monterosso and just below, the beach of Gùvano on the sea. We cross the tarmacked road several times before reaching Fornacchi, a nucleus consisting of a few houses surrounded by woods, vines, vegetable gardens and grassy strips which are periodically mown. Here we follow the road up and turn uphill at a bend

through a pinewood. The route runs alongside the Zuara meadow and joins an unmade road. Here we meet route 7b going steeply uphill from Corniglia.

We continue through the pinewood, marked by fires, on a wide bridle path for about a kilometre, first slightly uphill and then on level ground at an altitude of 600m, crossing one of the widest gorse formations in the Cinque Terre. We leave the bridle path, which continues upwards around the southern slopes of Mt. Gaginara and follow the flat path on the right; after a few hundred metres we reach the Cigoletta saddle. At this intersection route 1 leads left towards Mts. Gaginara and Malpertuso, and right towards Mt. Marvede and towards route 7a down to Corniglia; if, alternatively you continue with route 7, you will reach Casella and Riccò del Golfo in Val di Vara.

 Vernazza - Sanctuary of N. S. di Reggio - Foce Drignana

Route no.	8
Altitudes:	departure: 10
	arrival: 500 (maximum)
Height differences:	490 (ascent)
Length:	3 km
Difficulty:	slight
Time:	1 1/2 hours

This route is of cultural, religious and scenic interest, and reaches the old Reggio Sanctuary, linking the sea to the ridge path (which leads to Mt. Malpertuso, the highest in the Cinque Terre) in the quickest way possible.

Turn right immediately at the station and go uphill to the left as far as Via Brigate Partigiane (once Via dei Frati), where the first stations of the Via Crucis

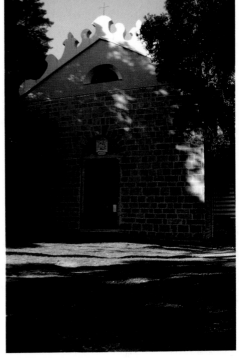

129 - *View from Reggio*
130 - *N. S. di Reggio*

are situated. Near the cemetery there is beautiful view of Vernazza with its towers, harbour and the multi-coloured terraces of houses. The paved route clambers up among olives and arrives at the chapel of S. Bernardo, where there is a bench to rest on before continuing uphill among olive groves and covered dry-stone walls with typical flora like stonecrops, navelwort, wall pellitory and spur-valerian. Here and there are large rocks with clear sub-vertical strata; across a small canal is a wide view of the Vernazza basin, the largest in the Cinque Terre. We encounter a house with vegetable plot, vines and olive grove, and after a short distance the shrine dedicated to S. Maria which indicates the end of the holy route.

We now reach the Reggio Sanctuary probably built in the 11th century on the ruins of an ancient place of prayer (p. 105). In an artificial cave cool water springs from three big marble masks: there is space to rest in the shade of majestic sophora, horse-chestnut, fir, cedar, thuja, linden and holm oak trees. Behind and above the sanctuary a short cut leads to a tarmacked road which we cross, and up on a path bending right in a mixed wood of pines, holm oak and chestnut with a thriving undergrowth of tree heath. Alongside the little Villa Giunzina, across farmlands and abandoned terraces, we reach the road again and follow it on the right; turn left at the first fork and right at the next, at you will at last reach Foce Drignana, one of the oldest passes between the coast and inland area. The scenic view shows Case Drignana and Reggio in the foreground, and further away S. Bernardino. Instead of turning, it is possible to continue along the provincial *via dei Santuari* which winds along the length of the Cinque Terre, but our route meets ridge route 1 before heading down towards Pignone in Val di Vara.

From Monterosso

Monterosso - Soviore Sanctuary
Route no. 9

Altitudes:	departure: 5
	arrival: 465 (maximum)
Height differences:	460 (ascent)
Length:	3 km
Difficulty:	slight
Time:	1¹ᐟ⁴ hours

This is a short walk of mainly cultural and religious interest, with paved sections in the woods; the route can join the *Via dei Santuari* and route 1.

From the station, follow the Fegina promenade to the left as far as the old village of Monterosso; take Via Roma as far as the parking area, and here follow a path uphill through little old houses and vegetable gardens enclosed in walls. Crossing a strip of holm oak wood we come out on the coastal road

131 - A chapel near Soviore
132 - The sea and Punta Mesco from Monterosso

near a bend, cross it, and pack up the path again upwards through the wood. There are a few shrines which emphasise the religious feeling of this route. Behind us is a scenic glimpse of Monterosso with the old walls and castle ruins above it. We encounter a chapel, rebuilt in 1865 on the ruins of an older small temple built to give thanks to Our Lady of Soviore after an epidemic. After a short distance through a mixed wood of holm oak, chestnut and pines,

118

the paved route reaches the sanctuary with its large square. the complex of buildings is imposing and the church, of ancient origins, was modified in the 14th and 18th centuries and again more recently. The portal and belltower are particularly attractive (p. 105).

The visit is enhanced by the shade of ancient holm oaks and the beautiful view over the Mesco promontory; a trattoria and lodge offer further possibilities of refreshment. The nearby tarmacked road coincides in this section with ridge route 1, which arrives to the west at Colla di Gritta and Termine to the east.

 ## Monterosso - Mesco (Semaforo)

Route no.	10
Altitudes:	departure: 5
	arrival: 313
	maximum: 315
Height differences:	312 (+310, -2)
Length:	2 km
Difficulty:	slight
Time:	45 minutes

This is a short uphill route amidst the maquis and a pine wood, with wide scenic views and interesting historical and environmental evidence. it is possible to continue towards Levanto or along the ridge on route 1.

Leaving the station follow the Fegina promenade to the right as far as the sailing club and the imposing Statue of a Giant, in reinforced concrete built in 1910 by the sculptor Arrigo Minerbi. We pass under a series of arches and near an large gabbro boulder, and zigzag uphill

first using steps, and then on a path alongside the Torre dei Merli. On the crags thyme, golden eternal flowers, spiny spurge and Luni cornflower stand out for their scent and colour. The serpentinites are visible and the maquis is a splendid mosaic of red juniper, mock privet, myrtle and lentisk

The path joins a tarmacked road, and after following this for a short section across a small saddle, we take a bridle path, with steps on the right, which passes alongside a hotel and into a thick pinewood. Ignore all other, lateral paths and continue upwards through maquis and a sparse pinewood until you reach the crest and ridge route 1. Now we turn sharply left on flat ground to reach the Semaforo del Mesco (Telegrafo) where in past centuries Saracen ships were sighted and signalled with the lighthouse. Here are the ruins, few but pleasant, of the old monastery of S. Antonio (p. 92) and a wide view which on a clear day includes the Maritime Alps.

133 - *The statue of the giant at Monterosso*
134 - *The coast towards to Portovenere and the islands*

Tramonti routes

 Campiglia - Albana (sea)

Route no.	11a
Altitudes:	departure: 400
	arrival: 0
	maximum: 403
Height differences:	406 (+3, -403)
Length:	1.3 km
Difficulty:	fairly
Time:	40 minutes

This route provides an opportunity for observation of a holm oak wood and the contact points between highly colourful geological formations of scientific interest. There is also a wonderful view towards Portovenere and the islands.

From Campiglia's small sports field, along

the road leading up from La Spezia, the route is the same as route 1, but then zigzags steeply downhill on a path in a thick holm oak wood. The heather bushes making up the maquis have been overwhelmed and scorpion senna, bushy spurges, hellebores and violets only flower in the sunniest clearings; in the undergrowth greater spleenworth, butcher's broom, prickly ivy and wild madder are common. When you reach the Fosso di Albana, you encounter several times an unmade road which has seriously undermined the continuity of the holm oak wood promoting the diffusion of rubble-loving species.

The route passes a modern building shaped like a castle, and rebuilt several times due to serious fires; it then crosses the Fosso passing to the opposite slope among pines, maquis bushes and fallow land. We go steeply downhill at a crest of Punta Persico arriving immediately to the west of Casa Boccardi: here there is the most spectacular view of the eastern Ligurian coast: to the west a spit of shingly beach, the Ferale cliffs and the points on which Schiara, Monesteroli and Fossola nestle, and to the east the Albana valley, the Galera crags and an imposing cliff stretching as far as Tino, almost imperceptibly interrupted by the inlets between the islands. At some points the cliffs reach 250m high but their spectacular nature is increased by the multicoloured juxtaposition of red and white rocks, spattered intermittently with green bushes clinging to the ledges.

Geologically speaking, various formations of the Tuscan series come into contact here representing the periods between the Rhaetian (more than 190 million years ago) and Oligocene (26 million years ago):

the white *Rhaetavicula contorta* limestone and solid limestone stretch from the east to Scoglio Galera, then in swift succession towards the Punta del Persico, *Angulata* limestones, ammonitic red limestone, flinty limestones, Posidonomya marls, jasper, majolica, multi-coloured shales and lastly the Macigno sandstones. The cliffs also represent important nesting or perching sites for rare birds, or those becoming rarer: the peregrine falcon, raven, pallid swift, the red-rumped swallow, blue rock thrush and various others.

Casa Boccardi at the bottom of the valley was built in the Napoleonic period probably on an ancient settlement belonging to the St. Venerio monastery of the island of Tino; the valley indicate the eastern limit of the production area of the DOC "Cinque Terre" and "Cinque Terre sciacchetrà" wines.

Further downhill, quite steeply, we reach the sea; from it is possible to swim to a small bridge under the red crag over Scoglio Galera, accessible only by sea, or continue towards the west along the cliffs towards the shingle beaches of Persico and Navone to come back up again on route 11.

 Campiglia - Punta del Persico

Route no.	*11*
Altitudes:	*departure: 400*
	arrival: 0
Height differences:	*400 (descent)*
Length:	*1.3 km*
Difficulty:	*fairly*
Time:	*40 minutes*

135 - *Persico*
136 - *The chapel of S. Antonio*

This route almost totally follows a characteristic flight of steps and offers the opportunity to observe particular features of the Tramonti area. The last section is hard going; before beginning this route it is a good idea to make sure you will be able to climb back up again.

At a restaurant in the square of Campiglia we begin our descent crossing a vast area of vines, some on trellises and some lying on the hot, dry ground. After passing through a group of pines and holm oak the route continues gently down steps on a rocky wall. The island of Tino is visible in the background. The path runs alongside Chioso, a partly-abandoned group of houses with olive grove. The path suddenly becomes steeper and follows a series of tight hairpin bends, between ever narrower cultivated terraces. On the dry-stone walls stonecrops, spur-valerian and golden golden eternal flowers grow. At a height of 220m there is a wider view; further down at Persico are the glowing red rooves of small huts where the people of Biassa tend to spend the summer. The steps cut from blocks of sandstone among abandoned vines and terraces often leave no space to place your feet; vine stalks, now wild, snake along small disconnected terraces almost as far as the sea. The maquis begins decisively to prevail with intense scents and pleasing splashes of colour: yellow Spanish broom, the changeable green of spurges, white flowering rock roses; between the stones are wall lizards, geckoes and long whip snakes try to hide from the people passing by. On the left the path for Valle di Albana branches off, while the steps become increasingly steep and difficult down to the sea. If you do not wish to return with the same route, it is possible to continue with necessary care along the rocks to join paths 11a and 4.

 ### Valico di S. Antonio - Schiara - sea

Route no.	4
Altitudes:	departure: 511
	arrival: 0
Height differences:	511 (descent)
Length:	2.6 km
Difficulty:	fairly
Time:	1 hour

The route offers many opportunities for natural and historical observation and to admire the wide views over the coast as far as Tino. The final section on the sea is difficult.

From the little church of S. Antonio Abate, go down a wide road through a pine and chestnut wood to a large stone set in a vertical position. This is the *menhir* of Tramonti, of prehistoric origin, but subsequently "Christianised" with the placing of the cross (recently removed). Opposite the *menhir* is a low wall built with long, heavy slabs, which was used in the past as a *posa* ("large stop"), where the baskets full of grapes from the harvest could be put down and the carrier rest his back.

We continue down to the right on a path through a wood dominated by holm oak, although pubescent oak and chestnut, and also a few corks, are plentiful. At 422m we meet a road; at the fork we turn left near a small house, among the vineyards (the right fork leads to Monesteroli). A little further on the islands of Palmaria and Tino can be seen and we go down again through a beautiful holm oak wood, to reach the Fontana di Nozzano, built during the presence of the Napoleonic soldiers watching over the La Spezia coast in 1805. When we reach the road at a hairpin bend, we follow it as shortly after it becomes a path. We cross well-kept vineyards with low walls and hedges of dry heather to protect from the wind and salinity. We go more steeply down a ridge with a marvellous view over the coast towards Palmaria and Tino; opposite, the Scoglio Ferale rises 26m out of the sea (a cross placed on it recalls the death of Lt. Luigi Garovaglio, who fell in 1911 during hydrographic surveys). We pass between the small houses of Schiara vertically arranged on the scarp: the rooves of the houses facing the sea are at road level and each one has a vegetable garden in front of the door. In summer, until grape harvest time, the people of Biassa and Campiglia move to these singular little settlements.

The menhir of Tramonti (one of which is in the Civic Museum of La Spezia) are considered by some experts to be among the most primitive expressions of the Lunigiana peoples who later produced a series of more or less worked "stone statues", now preserved in various museums. According to others they had a calendar function; it would seem that during the summer solstice the sun positioned the shadow of the menhir at the centre of the posa.

137 - The menhir of Tramonti

We then encounter the pretty white S. Antonio Oratory, and then the steps become very steep. After the last few houses heather, holm oak and especially tree-spurge dominate the landscape. The descent is difficult among rocks and stones, as far as the pretty Schiara shores, where large boulders alternate with shingle and coarse sand, and the sea is full of fish.

 Campiglia - Fossola - Campi

Route no.	4b
Altitudes:	departure: 400
	arrival: 258
Height differences:	262 (+60, -202)
Length:	4.4 km
Difficulty:	slight-fairly
Time:	1 1/2 hours

This highly scenic route which passes a few hundred metres above the sea allows you to wander over almost all the Tramonti coast with its vineyards and dry-stone walls. The first section is flat and easy-going,

although here and there are landslides, which are difficult to cross; the final section is on tarmac along the state highway. We leave Campiglia from the little square near a fountain: opposite Schiara and Scoglio Ferale are visible. We cross a few vineyards at the edge of the wood and then enter a cool pine wood with holm oak, chestnut and pubescent oak, where mountain species like the mountain cornflower and Piedmontese wood-rush can be seen, in contrast with cork oak, with its coarse wrinkly bark, and the rare oval bedstraw, both of which are western Mediterranean species at the northern limit of their habitat. The densest population of the cork oak in Liguria is here in this area between Campiglia, Valico di S. Antonio and the Fontana di Nozzano.

We go slightly downhill through well-tended vineyards, sometimes protected from the wind and salinity by heather hedges. Behind us Punta del Persico can be seen and further away the islands of Palmaria and Tino. We pass just above Schiara with its glowing red rooves, and reach the road down from Colle del Telegrafo to Schiara. We follow this downhill for a few metres to the next hairpin bend where we bear right through a thick holm oak wood to the Fontana di Nozzano of 1805. Having left the wide bridle path with steps which leads up to the Telegrafo, we take the flat path to the left through vineyards over a large landslide area. From this section which is highly scenic we can see almost all the Tramonti coast. We encounter route 4d with its convenient steps going down to Monesteroli and follow it on the ridge as far as 270m high near a monorail and a trigonometric post, where we can overlook

125

138 - Vines near Schiara and the Ferale crag on the sea

In any case we must go uphill as far as Casotti and on a short stretch of road or the path running parallel to it through tidy vineyards and small holm oak and pine woods, to reach the western mouth of the Biassa tunnel at a restaurant.

By following the state highway we can quickly reach Campi, a few houses scattered on a natural terrace, which along with the one in Volastra is the widest in the Cinque Terre. Once it was possible to follow the path from Campi to Riomaggiore passing above the Canneto bay, but now, as a result of the construction of the coast road, intensified landslide action has blocked this pedestrian route. From Campi we can go downhill with route 4h to Punta Pineda where, once, small wine barrels were loaded onto ships.

from on high the small group of houses forming Monesteroli.

A little lower down, instead of continuing on the steep flight of steps, we turn right on a flat path towards Fosso di Reboi in the dense maquis dominated by tree heath, arbutus and holm oak. The path is more difficult but it is worth the effort: over the sea we can see the inlet of Fossola and the beach of Nacchè; beyond the channel we cross vineyards, often abandoned, with dry-stone walls crumbling due to landslide. When we reach Fossola, along its channel, we continue on level ground as far as the flight of steps on the ridge of the Costa dell'Angelo, at the little white church of Angeli Custodi (Guardian Angels), or else go uphill to the right near the channel and rejoin this same flight of steps higher up.

 Valico di S. Antonio - Fossola - sea

Route no.	4c
Altitudes:	departure: 511
	arrival: 0
Height differences:	511 (descent)
Length:	1.4 km
Difficulty:	slight
Time:	40 minutes

This route, with steps, has a steep final section but is easy to follow throughout. There are many scenic points and opportunities for observation of nature.

We leave the little church of S. Antonio and the exercise route to head downhill towards the sea on route 4c, which is wide and well-paved, crossing a pine wood with tall maritime pines over a beautiful maquis of heather, arbutus and holm oak. The maquis sometimes reaches tree height and

139 - "Wine-cellars" at Fossola

reconstitutes the natural woodland. In the pine wood greater spotted woodpeckers, tree creepers, wrynecks, coal tits, squirrels and dormice can all be frequently seen.

Ignoring a path to the right, continue down through the wood where the path becomes a wide flight of steps, becoming steeper. At a bend, towers an old and imposing holm oak tree; the wood becomes sparser and gives way to vineyards. We continue down along the crest of the Costa degli Angeli with wide views over the houses of Fossola, Monesteroli, Campi and Pineda. We pass through Fossola and, having encountered path 4b, reach the pretty church of Angeli Custodi (Guardian Angels).

At a height of 200m, we come across a crag between Punta Merlino and the Fossola stream; to avoid it, the steps veer abruptly to the left and arrive at the last few houses of the village, from where they again head downhill steeply alongside the stream to the sea. It is possible, but a little difficult, to continue along the rocks to Punta Merlino, opposite which the Scoglio Grimaldo rises from the sea; otherwise, to the east, we can reach the Fossola bay and the beach of Nacchè, or further on, the mooring of Monesteroli with the Montonaio rocks, and from here climb up again on route 4d.

Valico di S. Antonio - Monesteroli - sea

Route no.	4d
Altitudes:	departure: 511
	arrival: 0
Height differences:	511 (descent)
Length:	2.2 km
Difficulty:	slight-fairly
Time:	1 hour

The route is identical to route 4 at the beginning, but then it branches off and becomes very steep, although it offers brief scenic views between the maquis and partly abandoned farmlands.

After seeing the *menhir* and the interesting cork oak population, we reach Pian Veo and leave the section in common with route 4; we go downhill on a well-paved route with steps on the Costa dei Pozai, deep in a shady holm oak wood. We meet the road again on the right and at a height of 345 m we leave the wood to enter vineyards partially reclaimed by the tree heath maquis.

On the left route 4b (Campiglia-Campi) joins us, and follows our steps for a short distance before branching off to the right, near the trigonometric pillar. Below us the houses of Monesteroli appear, with red rooves and white terraces, close together and deep in the green of maquis and vineyards, jutting over the blue of the sea. The steps become steeper and at times disconnected, and follows the crest through tree-spurge, heather, holm oak, agaves and spiny broom. On the dry-stone walls stonecrops, golden eternal flowers and rusty-back fern grow, and wall lizards and geckoes bask in the sun.

Monesteroli is ranged on the right down

140 - Punta Monesteroli

to 85m above the sea and gives a splendid view of Punta del Persico, Palmaria and Tino, and to the west, Punta di Montenero, hiding Riomaggiore and the Mesco promontory. Some experts claim that the name of this ancient village can be traced back to the Greek hero Menestheus, who inspired Achaean refugees to found a colony in the 8th century but many doubts surround this theory. Going steeply down on the west side of the point, right opposite the Montonaio rocks, we arrive at the sea among agaves, maritime cineraria and rock samphire. It is possible, but very difficult, to follow the beach of Nacchè and the Fossola bay along the rocks to go up again to the Costa degli Angeli on route 4c.

141 - The Levanto promenade

Levanto routes

 ### Levanto - Punta Mesco

Route no.	*1*
Altitudes:	*departure: 2*
	arrival: 320
	maximum: 324
Height differences:	*412 (-365, -47)*
Length:	*5 km*
Difficulty:	*slight*
Time:	*1³/⁴ hours*

Characteristics: offers wide scenic views and opportunities for nature observation; the route follows the main ridge of the Cinque Terre and beyond as far as Portovenere. For the description, refer to the reverse route described as the final leg of the route crossing the Cinque Terre ridge (p. 93).

When the route reaches the intersection with route 10, turn right and follow the ridge for a few hundred metres as far as the ruins of the old S. Antonio monastery (see p.93).

 ### Levanto - Colle di Gritta

Route no.	*12*
Altitudes:	*departure: 2*
	arrival: 330 (maximum)
Height differences:	*328 (ascent)*
Length:	*4 km*
Difficulty:	*slight*
Time:	*50 minutes*

The route follows a tarmacked road at

142 - *Legnaro*

the valley bottom and then an easy bridle path, passing through an ancient settlement and joining ridge route 1. At the destination refreshment is available at a trattoria.

From the station, we pass below the railway, cross a bridge on the Ghiararo and go up the valley, initially following the watercourse on the left. We follow the road to Monterosso for a long section, which crosses the Ghiararo and leads us gradually up the opposite slope below Ridarolo and Legnaro, birthplace of Domenico Viviani, famous botanist of the early 19th century and founder of Genoa University's Botanical Gardens. After we cross the stream, route 18 branches off up to Poggio Bardellone. Notice how the small alluvial plain behind Levanto has been used for vegetable gardens, while the slopes exposed to the south are covered in olive groves and vines; contrastingly woods,

mainly of pine and chestnut, cover the cooler north facing slopes. Along the drainage lines alder, poplar, willow and hornbeam flourish, while the sunnier prominences are dominated by holm oak. At the first hairpin bend we leave the main road, turn right and continue for about 400m. When we finally leave the valley bottom, we cross the watercourse on a bridge at the old mill of Chiesanuova, go up to the left on a bridle path which cuts through beautiful olive groves and reaches the square of Fontona. This is a small village, set around the ridge, probably founded by the Longobards. According to some writers its original name was Friedenzona. An old mill can be seen on the Ghiararo and other settlements on the slopes, like case Trinchetto, Chiesanuova, and Legnaro. We continue uphill on the bridle path which draws near to the ridge and after about 300m we reach a fork: the path to the right leads to the small church of Madonna del Soccorso but we go straight on in a mixed wood of pine and broadleaf trees, until the hairpin bend of a steep road leading uphill. We now follow this road and after a few hundred metres reach the Colla di Gritta at the hotel-restaurant. Here the roads pass for Levanto, Monterosso and Pignone, and the ridge route 1 with which we can continue towards Punta Mesco, or along the road to Soviore.

 Levanto - Colla dei Bagari

Route no.	22
Altitudes:	departure: 0
	arrival: 360 (maximum)
Height differences:	358 (ascent)
Length:	2.8 km
Difficulty:	slight

143 - Chiesanuova

Time: 1 hour
This very scenic route is of historical and natural interest. It joins ridge route 1, on which we can reach Punta Mesco and double back to end the excursion, or continue to Monterosso.

The route leads uphill alongside the village walls, built in the 13th century, as far as the clock tower, and then between high walls on an old, important bridle path continuing up through olive groves and vineyards. While crossing the Monte delle Forche ridge, which separates the small Cantarana and Sella valleys, various agricultural settlements can be seen. The Rio Cantarana valley, which runs parallel to the coastline, is sunny and yet sheltered from the wind, but in particular it has in the past provided a better defence from Saracen invasions, as it is not visible from the sea. At 150m high, ignore the path leading to the left down to Levanto;

a little further on the bridle path becomes easier and reaches Palazzetto: here a road leads down towards Rio Sella and arrives in Levanto at the hospital, while to the left, near a house, another path crosses the Rio Cantarana and joins route 14. We must however go straight on, first on the ridge and then on the southern slopes of the Costa Sopramare. The landscape is dominated by olives and maritime pine; the geological substratum characterised by Bracco ophiolites and their coverings (lherzolites, gabbros and Palombini shales) strongly conditions the flora housing species particularly suited to ground poor in nutritive substances, but rich in magnesium and nickel like the exclusive Ligurian lavender cotton, the serpentine plantain, Salzmann's greenweed, strong-leafed fescue. We reach the Colla dei Bagari, almost on level ground where we join ridge route 1 at the point where route 14 arrives, also on its way up from Levanto.

 Levanto - Case Baldoria - Monte Vè

Route no.	15
Altitudes:	departure: 2
	arrival: 486 (maximum)
Height differences:	484 (ascent)
Length:	3 km
Difficulty:	slight
Time:	1 3/4 hours

This first section of this highly scenic route is identical to route 1; it arrives at the highest point of Mesco Promontory from where it is possible to double back and end the excursion with routes 14 or 16. From the promenade, we go up a flight of steps following route 1 towards the Medieval castle and onwards as far as the Mesco coast road, at Casa Farraggiana. Here we leave route 1 and follow the road to the left. After a short distance we turn right onto a road leading steeply up with several bends to Casa Baldoria at 270m high. There is a splendid view over the whole Levanto valley and western coast of Mesco. We continue upwards through pines and bushes of maquis to Piano di Seghezza, from where we continue almost on level ground deep in a sparse pine wood which offers scenic glimpses here and there. On the left is a path which leads along flat ground to Colla dei Bagari, but we continue steeply up on the ridge to the peak of Monte Vè, where route 14 joins us.

 Levanto - Prealba - Monte Vè

Route no.	14
Altitudes:	departure: 2
	arrival: 486 (maximum)
Height differences:	484 (ascent)
Length:	2.9 km
Difficulty:	slight
Time:	1 3/4 hours

This is an easy route encountering several points of historical and natural interest, following the old council road linking Levanto to Monterosso. It meets ridge route 1 and it is possible to double back and return with routes 15 or 22.

At the beginning of the route note the 13th century walls with watch tower. We follow the Cantarana stream, cross an old bridge and go up the left hand slope of

144 - *Levanto: the medieval walls and the clock tower*

145 - The Levanto valley

the valley. At Prealba a small road leads us to the Mesco coast road which we follow for only a few metres before entering another road which arrives among the olives at Casa Missionario. Alternatively, just below, still on the left slope of Val Cantarana, the old path (often blocked by vegetation) also leads to Casa Missionario. From here, proceed among pines and maquis bushes to the Tiro a Segno, encountering a path on the right leading to the beautiful farmhouse of Casa Vivaro della Merla, surrounded by olives and abandoned terraces. Route 14 continues however, parallel to Rio Cantarana. We begin to go steeply uphill, reaching a small trigonometric post and an iron and copper mine. The more open areas, among maritime pines, show particular

and interesting aspects of vegetation, almost exclusively linked to ophiolitic substrata: this is a pseudo-garrigue with Salzmann's greenweed, Ligurian lavender cotton, golden eternal flowers, small pinks etc. Where the soil avoids being washed away and manages to evolve, maquis develops which prepares the rooting of the holm oak wood. After a short distance we reach Colla dei Bagari, a crossroads with ridge route 1 and the arrival point of route 22 which descends to Fontona and Levanto. We turn right going uphill steeply along the ridge and shortly reach the peak of Monte Vè. From here we can return to Levanto on route 15 which follows the north-western Mesco ridge in a scenic position.

Levanto - Poggio Bardellone

Route no.	18
Altitudes:	departure: 2
	arrival: 613 (maximum)
Height differences:	651 (+631, -20)
Length:	4.5 km
Difficulty:	slight
Time:	2 hours

This route follows the St. Matthew coast, location of ancient medieval settlements and arrives at the ridge marking the boundary of the Levanto valley, linking up with a good trekking route; there are many scenic views and elements of natural interest.

The first part of the route is the same as route 12, but it branches off from it after crossing the bridge on the Ghiararo stream. We follow a steep flight of steps up through vines, vegetable gardens and green olive groves, as far as Ridarolo, a Medieval centre perched on a ridge; the only remaining original feature is the 13th century church. We bear left on almost level ground, on the cool slope facing the Rio Ghiare, and among the olives reach the Casa del Barone, or else we can follow the ridge along the aqueduct; on the valley bottom are the ancient ruins of the church of S. Matteo. We go up to Poggio S. Bartolomeo leaving behind farmlands and entering a wood of pine and chestnut, oaks, manna ash, and hop-hornbeam. When we arrive at the Traine fountain, a steep uphill section with small hairpin bends leads us to the Sascio spring (most spring water is collected and used to supply the aqueducts of Levanto and its surrounding area). We continue up in the cool chestnut and holm oak wood to a fork; here route 17a leads to the right towards the chapel of Foce S. Antonio, while our route 18 turns sharply left and arrives gently at Poggio Bardellone, whose name derives from the Longobard "bridilo" (= strip), joining the ridge road which links the Cinque Terre to the Apennine ridge. To the right we can get to Foce S. Antonio, Foce di Legnaro and further on the Soviore sanctuary; to the left is Case Vagine, from the Longobard "gahagi" (=reserved land), an important inn and horse changing station in the 18th century. This area is the site of pre-Ligurian archaeological findings proving the existence of an important communication route between the coast and the inland area along a dominant position of the ridge. Also situated on Monte Bardellone are the ruins on the medieval castle of Celasco, with the ruins of a round tower. There are scenic glimpses of the Levanto valley and the Rio Casale basin, which flows into the Vara.

Levanto - Montale

Route no.	24
Altitudes:	departure: 2
	arrival: 167 (maximum)
Height differences:	165 (ascent)
Length:	1.8 km
Difficulty:	slight
Time:	40 minutes

This is a short walk to a small town of ancient origins, with plenty of scenic views. Leaving the station we pass under the railway and along the valley bottom; on the right is the watercourse of Ghiararo and then its main influent, Rio Ghiare.

146 - Montale

We arrive at S. Antonio where archaeological traces of a late-ancient or early medieval settlement can be seen, and where preRoman tombs were found. We leave the tarmacked road, which leads towards the ancient settlements of Pastine and Vignana, and go uphill to the left along the ridge, through terraces covered with olives, and after a short distance we reach Montale to admire the magnificent Parish church.

The Parish church of S. Siro in Montale di Levanto is a place of worship and a place of historical interest halfway up the slope (like the Cinque Terre sanctuaries) which is definitely worth visiting. This is an 11th century protoRomanesque church built over the old fortalice of Ceula, suing the pre-existent tower. The facade is 18th century but the interior has been almost entirely restored to its medieval appearance, by removing the subsequent layers. Of note near the church is the S. Croce (Holy Cross) oratory with a beautiful 16th century portal. Ceula, a small town, which has helped found many others in the area, was on an important preRoman line of communication.

From the town we can continue up along the crest crossing the small groups of houses of Sorlana and Loreto, as far as Foce di Montale, a pass overlooking Val di Vara.

 Levanto - Bonassola

Altitudes:	departure: 2
	arrival: 7
	maximum: 165
Height differences:	321 (+163, -208)
Length:	3 km
Difficulty:	slight
Time:	1 hour

This short walk along the coast is the ideal way to follow the scenic blue route of the Cinque Terre; it is possible to choose between several variations, some of which venture further inland, and one close to the sea.

We reach the western end of Levanto's promenade, built on the former railway head office, and just before the old tunnel we go uphill to the right on a flight of steps deep in the greenery of villas and gardens. The route crosses stretches of pinewood and attractive maquis and

147 - Vines and olive groves between Levanto and Bonasola